THEY CALL ME MOM

By

Kelly

Table of Contents

Dedication i

Acknowledgments...ii

About the Author iii

Prologue 1

Epilogue 104

Footnotes 111

Timeline 127

Dedication

This book is dedicated to every woman who has loved and nurtured the child of another woman.

II Corinthians 1:3-4

"Praise be to the God and Father of our Lord Jesus Christ, the Father of compassion and the God of all comfort, who comforts us in all our troubles, so that we can comfort those in any trouble with the comfort we ourselves receive from God."

Acknowledgments

Ten years ago my daughter asked me to record my memories of our time as foster parents. I agreed, not realizing the enormity of what I would be taking on. I'm not a writer but I began to jot things down. As I recalled the children and their stories it was like living through it all over again. I would often set it aside for periods of time, sometimes years, but always came back to it. After I finally completed my manuscript I was encouraged to share it outside our family. So here it is, my joy, my sorrows, my life.

About the Author

Kelly McFarland is an adult child from hard places. She decided early in her life to be a champion for children because she was often a child in need of a champion. She has dedicated her life to investing in people, particularly children, her own by birth, adoption, and kinship and those that she made her own through the foster care system. Kelly also has worked in summer camps for at risk children and in orphanages in Uganda. These days she has no children in her home except when the grandchildren are over. She lives with her three dogs, her husband, and her 11 goats in the great state of Texas.

Prologue

"How many kids do you have?" Every time I hear this simple question, I have to stop and figure out how to answer. The easy answer is two, but if I want to include Lacy, then I have to explain who she is. If I include my foster babies, then it becomes a much longer conversation. Depending on the person and the relationship, I have to choose what to reveal.

Over the years, God gave me many children; perfect children, broken children, abused children, neglected children, abandoned children, rejected children, and despised children. I loved them all. They call me Mom.

The winter I turned 17, I met my best friend. He was funny; he challenged me and believed I was someone special. I married him in the fall of 1980.

Dean and I spent our early years together, playing and enjoying our little family of dogs and birds. We rafted rivers, went fishing, camping, sledding, shooting and exploring Alaska together.

1982

After a couple of years of married life, I became pregnant. I was working at an oil company in Anchorage and Dean was working with a crew on the North Slope. He was out of town for weeks, sometimes months, at a time with no way to reach him other than the mail. So I wrote him a letter and told him he was going to be a Daddy. He immediately felt that it would be a girl. I personally didn't care either way.

From the moment that test proved my suspicions, I was sick. I had day-long morning sickness for months. Although the pregnancy was rough, I was excited. I grew up with a single parent who was narcissistic and abusive. I was determined that my baby would have a different type of childhood. She would be surrounded by people who loved her. Her needs would be met, and she would know what a precious gift she was.

As I went about my life at work and home, I would talk to my bump and tell her all the wonderful things she had to look forward to. I told her how much she was loved and how excited I was to be her Mom.

In the third trimester, I developed toxemia. I was so swollen I could only wear flip flops, in Alaska, in November. The doctor put me on bed rest, and I was frustrated because I wanted to get her room set up and get myself organized for her arrival. As it was, I got to lay on my side while I watched Dean do all the work.

My doctor finally hospitalized me because of my blood pressure, and I was put on Pitocin to get things moving. After three days with no progress, they broke my water and started labor with more Pitocin. Eight hours later, the little lady made her appearance. Due to complications, her pediatrician was called in. He arrived just in time, wearing a tuxedo. Michelle had the cord around her neck three times and wasn't breathing. She was handed off to Dr. Lyon, and everyone held their breath. Then she let out a little cry, and everything was good. I finally got to meet my long-awaited, deeply loved, precious daughter.

As she grew, Michelle introduced Dean and me to so many new experiences. When she was about six weeks old, she got the first of many ear infections. She then started to projectile vomit. It was amazing to see unless you were in the line of fire. She could cover everything within a 4' radius. She was on antibiotics for months. At three months, she picked up viral pneumonia from her daycare. Watching her in a misting tent with an IV in her head was devastating to me. Dean and I started looking for an alternative to daycare.

We eventually arranged for her to stay with Dean's sister while he was up north and I was at work. It worked out pretty well. She got to spend her days playing with her cousins, Mike, Tricia, Sam and Lacy, and being around family. The really good part was that she was finally healthy.

Michelle was always a Daddy's girl. From the day she was born, she was the apple of his eye. No matter who else was there, including me, she wanted her Daddy. When he was home, she stayed with him and would often "help" him do things around the house. She helped him cook, she helped him go to the dump, and she helped him change the oil in the car. She was her Daddy's little helper, following him around in her little Osk Kosh coveralls with tools in her hands, and he loved it.

As she grew, she showed us her boundless confidence in herself and her faith in God. She prayed the sinner's prayer at three and began to intercede for family, friends and strangers. She was totally confident in God answering her prayers and would share Him with anyone and everyone she encountered. She would even make Dean and I pull off the road while driving so we could pray for someone. Bedtime prayers often turned into heavy intercession. She was really intense.

People were drawn to Michelle almost from the time she was born. I would find mothers holding her instead of their own children in the nursery. It was right on the edge of creepy. She just had something about her that people wanted to be around. She often said things that I thought would offend people, but they just accepted what she said and loved her regardless. She was incredibly black and white in her thoughts, and it never occurred to her to be anything else.

Dean worked on the slope for weeks and sometimes months at a time. So when he was home, she was pretty possessive of him and his time. She resented the attention I took away from her and showed it. She would squeeze between us on the sofa, break our hands apart while walking, and ask Dean if they had to bring me on outings.

When it came time for Dean to fly north for work, it was a nightmare. She would scream and fight me as I tried to leave the airport. I fully expected to be detained by airport police to prove I was her mother.

I don't want it to sound like she didn't love me because she did, and she showed it all the time. I just think because he was gone so much, she felt like she had to fight for every minute she could get.

1984

Michelle was such a joy that Dean and I decided to have another baby. I had already decided on six kids, and I hoped the next one would be a boy. I looked forward to having the Mother/Son relationship with him that I'd heard about from other mothers.

Unfortunately, it didn't happen. I consulted the doctor, and he started me on infertility treatments.

Infertility is a difficult condition to explain to someone who hasn't been through it themselves. Even Dean, though he tried, didn't really understand the depth of it. When you're told you can't have a child, it can become an obsession. It absolutely consumes you. It took me to dark places. I felt like a complete failure as a woman. I resented other women who could get pregnant, especially those who complained about it. I quit going to baby showers and working in the nursery. Even the Christmas Wish Book brought me to tears as I looked at those cherubic little faces. I understood the cries of Rachel and Hannah, who longed for a baby.

People often said, "Well, at least you have Michelle." but they didn't understand. I knew Michelle was a blessing, and I adored her, but the ache continued.

One day when I picked up Michelle after work, she greeted me with, "Hi, Aunt Kelly," and I felt completely defeated. I felt like I was losing her as well. With Dean out of town and me working an hour away in Anchorage, I was gone a lot. I didn't like the way our life was headed.

1985

We started looking for a new job for Dean, and surprisingly he was offered one in Ketchikan. Dean's dad lived there and agreed to help us with housing if we moved down. It meant big changes, including finances, family, and general lifestyle.

Dean went down first, and Michelle and I stayed behind to settle things. I quit my job, dealt with the house and packed everything up with the help of Dean's family. Margie, his mom, and I drove the vehicles to Haines, where we boarded the ferry to our new life in Ketchikan.

Ketchikan is an island in SE Alaska. The year-round population at that time was around 9000. It is also a rainforest with approximately 120" of annual rainfall. Dean's new job was at the pulp mill where a lot of the residents worked, including many of his childhood friends and Papa, his Dad.

Ketchikan has one main road about 30 miles long, with the city in the center. We lived on the north end of town in Knudson Cove. This is the same piece of property where Dean lived most of his childhood. Our house was on a hill and overlooked the cove and the Pacific Ocean.

When we moved, we moved into Papa's house and he took an apartment in town. He was so excited to have family around again and really helped us get settled.

There were a lot of adjustments, especially for Michelle and me. I was home all day, and Dean was home every evening. Everything around us was new and very different. I had never lived near the ocean and definitely not in a rain-forest. Michelle never had me at home full time and her dad home every night. It was all a bit unsettling for her. At first, she wanted me to go back to work so her dad could be home, but eventually, we all adjusted and settled into our new lives.

Michelle especially loved being around her Papa. They became very close and spent many happy hours together. He introduced her to coffee and some old-time logger sayings that got her in trouble at school later on.

I homeschooled Michelle in Kindergarten, and we both enjoyed it. She was smart, and I found that I really enjoyed teaching. Her only frustration was that I kept teaching her letter sounds instead of just telling her how to read! Patience wasn't really her thing.

For first grade, we put her in KCA, a private Christian school. She did well, but we did get a few phone calls. That black-and-white personality, her confidence, and those old-school sayings of Papa's got us both in trouble.

1989

When Michelle was six, we finally gave up on fertility treatments. We accepted that it simply wasn't going to happen naturally. We still believed we were meant to work with children and knew we couldn't afford adoption, so we began to look at foster care. We ideally thought we could offer a stable environment for a needy child, and both the state and the child would be thankful - idealism at its best.

We began the process with blinders on. We thought they'd be appreciative and help us to help a needy child. That's not really how it goes. The first thing you have to do is jump through all the hoops known as getting licensed. It is the most invasive process I've ever been through. They asked questions about my motives, my background, our marriage, our sex life, my religious beliefs, my ideas on discipline, my hygiene, my diet, and so on. I began to feel like I knew nothing. I don't have a discipline ideology, and if I told them about my childhood, they'd never approve of us. It's overwhelming. I felt like everything about me was wrong, but I answered their questions and hoped for the best. Then came the inspection. I believed our house was reasonably safe, but they found several things we needed to correct before they would approve it. So we took their list and made all the recommended changes.

We started to feel optimistic. Then came the re-inspection, and they found things they missed the first time. So, we went back to the store for the outlet covers, the cabinet locks and whatever else they thought of. We began to wonder if this was going to work out. Then out of the blue, we were approved and welcomed to the family of foster parents.

Just as we were in the last stages of getting licensed, I was approached by a friend from church. She worked at the hospital and knew about a baby who needed a foster home. She told me he was physically deformed and wanted to know if Dean and I would consider fostering him. She then drew me a picture on a napkin.

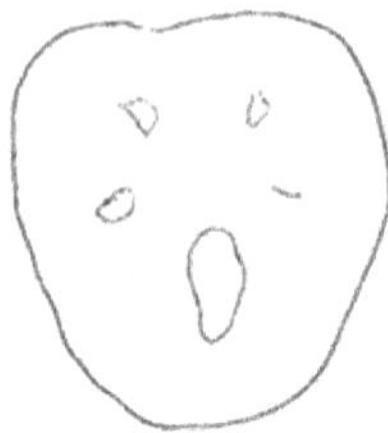

The picture was unbelievable. It couldn't be a real baby; it was more like an alien. I told her, "no." I absolutely couldn't do that. Nonetheless, I took the picture home and shared it with Dean. I was relieved when he agreed with me that this was completely outside of our abilities. Dean is such a nice guy and genuinely cares about everyone, so I was a little anxious about telling him in case he thought we should consider it. However, when he said "No," I felt like I could breathe easier.

During the following week, we often talked about the "baby" and his situation, but it always ended with some statement re-confirming that this wasn't the child for us. Yet, we couldn't get him out of our minds. Finally, after about a week, Dean looked at me, and we both knew. He asked if I'd give them a call, and I said yes.

The woman I spoke to, JoAnna, was the director at Community Connections. She told me a lot of things were still being worked out, and it was likely he wouldn't need a foster home. I told her that if things changed, we were available. It looked like the decision had been made for us, and I won't deny that I was relieved. It wasn't just his appearance. It was the whole idea of taking care of a baby you knew was going to die. How did you get up every morning, knowing this might be the day? How did you protect your heart from that kind of pain?

It wasn't long before we got the call. The situation was that Jacob had been born five months previous and was still in the hospital. The parents were initially told he was terminal and would likely die within hours or days at best.

As his life continued, decisions were made for his comfort and the ease of his caregivers. He was initially fed through an <u>orogastric tube</u>. As he got older, a <u>G-tube</u> was inserted to make things easier. His parents wanted him put into an institution in Juneau, but there wasn't an opening. They believed he needed full-time nursing care. The hospital disagreed and threatened to report him as abandoned if they didn't remove him. Kim, his mother, didn't believe any foster family would take him but agreed that if one could be found, she would agree to a voluntary placement until she could find a more suitable home for him. She signed all the paperwork under protest and made it very clear that she would fight this all the way.

That's where we came in. Kim was furious that a home was willing to take Jacob. She reluctantly agreed that we could meet him and make preparations to bring him home. Kim insisted that she be there when we met Jacob for the first time. We were apprehensive because we knew she was angry and weren't sure what kind of reception we would receive.

JoAnna led us to his room. There was a big "No Visitors" sign posted outside. We were told that Kim insisted that no one see Jacob except the necessary hospital staff. When we walked in, Kim was sitting in a rocking chair with her mother and husband standing behind her. The room was stark - nothing colorful or happy, no mobile or toys. No one spoke to us. They just stared as we walked across to Jacob's crib. When we got there, we saw that misshapen little face and his overlarge head. He was dressed in only a diaper. He had a tube coming out of his stomach, and it had a syringe in it. This was taped to the side of the crib with the formula in it. Jacob was laying perfectly still. His little feet were <u>clubbed,</u> and you could see places on his fingers where it looked like strings were tied around them. As I spoke to him, he began to stir. I reached down and held his little hand, and he tightened his fingers around mine. It wasn't instant acceptance, but something stirred in me. I couldn't help but be moved by this poor baby in this cold, sterile room.

After Kim, George and Claire left, we spent the afternoon with Jacob. The nursing staff was amazing once the family left. They interacted with Jacob and were really excited that he was going to have someone take care of him. They told me that Kim wanted us to spend two weeks learning about Jacob's care, but it wasn't necessary. They showed us how to feed him and even had me do his next feed while they observed. Then they explained that if his tube popped out, we needed to get him to the hospital as soon as possible as the hole would begin to close up. Then they explained about his <u>fixed shunt</u>.

Jacob was born with <u>hydrocephalus</u>. A shunt was inserted weeks prior, and it slowly drained off excess cerebral fluid, reducing the pressure inside his head. The only thing we needed to watch out for was the unlikely event it became clogged. Unless he ran a fever, we should assume it was working fine. His forehead wasn't bone; it was displaced cartilage that should have formed his nose. As the pressure in his head decreased, his forehead sunk in. It was a little shocking the first time I saw it, but perfectly normal for Jacob.

He was basically <u>anencephalic</u>, with only a small bit of brain matter sitting on the top of his brain stem. He had a <u>mid-facial cleft</u>. His nose was missing, and his nares were on his forehead. His upper palate was vertical rather than horizontal. This made feeding him orally impossible. He was, for all intents and purposes, blind. His one eye didn't have any bone around it and was just floating, like a balloon on a string. It was sunken in, and the eyelid didn't open. The assumption was that it would atrophy and never be of any use. His other eye was abnormally attached and looked upwards rather than forward. It also had a <u>coloboma</u>, so there were questions about what he could see, if anything. His feet were clubbed with fused toes. His hands showed signs of <u>amniotic banding</u>. He was kind of a mess.

Jacob's daily care was pretty basic other than the feedings and care of the g-tube. Since he couldn't suck on a nipple, we stimulated his digestive juices by rubbing a glycerin swab around his mouth at feeding times. He loved them and would get excited when he felt them in his mouth. They also helped to clean his mouth since he was a mouth breather and tended to have bad breath. Jacob had to be elevated when he was fed. Otherwise, the formula went into his stomach and right out his mouth. This caused a serious risk of aspiration. His g-tube site required special care as well. It usually had granulated tissue around it and wept a bit.

We were told that as Kim and George had signed a DNR, there would be no vaccinations, no preventive care, only what was needed for his comfort. We were advised not to get attached. Just give him basic care and call the doctor when he dies.

All of this was overwhelming. I felt really inadequate and doubted my ability to deal with everything. Jacob, the prospect of him dying in our care, and the family's hostility was a lot. Then there was the medical side and so much to remember about his care. Of course, there was also the paperwork, the case workers, and all the rest.

After all the paperwork was signed, the instructions were given, and the warnings were given again, we took Jacob home. JoAnna came to the house with us to get him settled.

After we hauled him and his adaptive equipment (bath chair, wedges, etc.) into the house, we laid Jacob on our bed to change him. That was when Michelle arrived. A friend had watched her while Dean and I were at the hospital.

Our bedroom window looked out on the walkway to the front door so she could see into the room as she approached. I remember her stopping and taking everything in. When she came in, she asked a few questions while observing Jacob but never really reacted. She just accepted him.

The first morning with Jacob, I woke up and there was a low-hanging cloud in my room. It took me a minute to remember that it was the humidifier that Jacob needed to keep his mouth and nares moist. Then it hit me again, all the emotions I had about this little boy who was denied love because he was different. As I got up, I once again fought with my doubt about being able to care for this sweet baby who needed me. Fortunately, it didn't take long until these doubts disappeared, and taking care of Jacob became part of our daily lives.

That evening I lay Jacob on a blanket and watched him play with his koosh ball. Every time he dropped it below his incision line, he acted like it was lost. When it was handed back to him, he would coo and mouth it. As I watched him, I made a decision. I could not stay detached from this baby who had already lived five months in isolation. He had never been loved, cuddled, or nurtured. His entire life had been as a medical oddity to be observed and studied. I went, sat by Jacob, and played koosh ball with him. I tickled him and caressed his sweet little cheeks. I held his hand and talked to him. I began to fall in love with this strange little person God brought into our lives. My mother's heart struggled with remaining detached and eventually I decided it just wasn't me. I knew I would pay for it later, but Jacob had lost too much already. Oddly enough, when I opened up and let Jacob in, so did Michelle and Dean. It was the most natural thing in the world.

Jacob brought many new people into our lives. His daily life was a whirlwind of activity. Initially, it was the caseworkers, respite, parents and home health. Later it included physical therapy, occupational therapy, vision specialists, infant learning, and doctors. It seemed like we either had people coming to the house or an appointment with some clinic or other on a regular basis.

Jacob's anomaly was so unique that there were only a couple of other recorded cases in which both babies died shortly following birth. There were always questions about what caused it. The answer is no one knows. There are lots of theories, but since it wasn't genetic, they remain theories.

Jacob, for all his issues, was the happiest baby. He loved music, so we would prop him up so his one functioning eye could see the television while Disney movies played. Even though we were told he couldn't see, we weren't sure we agreed. Eventually, we saw his eye was tracking Michelle's brightly colored teddy bear and began to do whatever we could to encourage it.

One of the things I had to do right off the bat was shop for Jacob. He came with very few clothes and no basic baby stuff. Michelle and I went to town and got everything we could think of. We bought him cute clothes, a stroller with a sunroof, a snugglie, a baby book and all sorts of toys. When we got home, Michelle was excited to dress him up like one of her baby dolls. I started working on his baby book. My intention was to keep it for myself, so I filled it with things from the hospital (id bracelet, baby stocking cap), a lock of hair from his first haircut, pictures, and notes about his development.

When I took Jacob to church to meet Pastor W, it was instant chemistry. Pastor loved Jacob, and Jacob loved him. Actually, Jacob was drawn to all men. Unfortunately, most of them took a bit to accept him. Most people accepted Jacob at a distance, and that was fine. There were a few who completely accepted him, and they were invaluable. Others just couldn't deal with him, and we lost friends. It was especially hard because we were already going through so much.

Dean always had a warped sense of humor and looked for ways to make light of Jacob's abnormalities. It wasn't that he didn't love him; it was just his way of coping. One day Jacob rolled off the pew at church, and Dean said, "Well, at least he can't break his nose." Another time, a woman walked into the nursery with her little girl and saw Dean feeding Jacob. They both stopped in the doorway and stared. Dean told the little girl that this was how we got Jacob to eat his vegetables.

After a couple of weeks, Kim called. She was going to be in town and wanted to see Jacob. We met in a parking lot and sat with the vehicle door open while she "visited" Jacob. There was no interest in him as a person, no touching, not even talking to him personally, just about him. She always wanted to know everything that was being done or talked about with therapists, doctors and Community Connections. It was at this visit that I finally began to see why she was so angry. She told us that Jacob was going to be named Zachariah, which means blessed of God, but when she saw him, she changed his name to Jacob, which means deceiver. She said she got pregnant but didn't get a baby.

We heard from friends that the parents told everyone at home that the baby died at birth. I tried to be understanding because they were told that he was terminal and his situation was complicated. It would have been overwhelming to try and explain it to an entire community. However, when I looked at him and cared for him, I knew I could not have dismissed him in this way.

When you live in a small community, it seems like everyone knows everyone else or at least has heard about them. It didn't take long before we heard the story of Jacob's birth.

When Kim went into labor, she came to Ketchikan from her hometown. She wasn't progressing, so they did an x-ray and saw enough to know there were serious problems. They did a C-section and swiftly removed him for evaluation. Kim and George were told that he was critical and would not live. If they wanted to see him, they should do it quickly. After Kim recovered, they returned home and told people he had died at birth. I'm sure it was easier than explaining about his condition. It's also easier to accept sympathy than pity. They were told Jacob would not live and saw no reason to question it.

As Jacob continued to live, Kim came back and forth to deal with medical decisions as she worked towards finding a nursing home that would take him. I'm sure it was hard on her, but it was hard on Jacob too.

After Kim's visit with Jacob, she sent a note and said she didn't want him out in public without her permission. We were floored. She wanted us to send her a list of the places we went to regularly, and she would decide where Jacob could go. She gave us permission to go to medical appointments and church. It was pretty ridiculous, but we tried to abide by it for a few weeks then we said no, we weren't going to ask her permission to live our lives. I felt certain she was still trying to keep him a secret, and people were beginning to talk. We got letters from Jacob's doctor, case workers, and therapists, who all agreed it was best for his well-being to be included in any and all available activities. Being out in the world was no threat to him, and the stimulus was great for his development. She reluctantly agreed, and life was calm for a bit.

Shortly after we got Jacob, we were introduced to the Aunties, G & C. These two precious women were special education teachers who also did respite care. They started watching Jacob for us, and we quickly became fast friends. They both loved Jacob and were such a blessing to us. They made it possible for us to have time off from all the drama that was Jacob's life. They gave us the gift of acceptance. They laughed with us at our unique situation and offered a shoulder to cry on. They let us rant without judgment and loved us through some ugly times. They gave us unconditional love and true friendship. Auntie G also gave us the most important tool to help us deal with all of the issues we faced with Jacob. She gave us permission to laugh at ourselves, Jacob and everything else.

The Aunties not only cared for Jacob, but they also became a huge support for Michelle as well. They were a gift to our family.

Jacob spent time with the Aunties, where he was spoiled without measure, and we were able to spend time with Michelle. She was such a help during this time, and it was great to be able to focus solely on her occasionally. I don't believe she resented Jacob, but her life drastically changed when he came. She had been an only child who had her parents' full attention. When Jacob came, she had a lot of adjusting to do. Fortunately, Papa lived next door, and he and

Michelle spent a lot of time together. He was able to give her the time and attention we didn't always have.

Whenever we took Jacob anywhere, we got looks. He was so unusual that people couldn't help but stare. When I just wasn't up to it, I would put him in his stroller, hang a blanket over the front, and keep an eye on him through the sunroof. I often took Jacob shopping like this because it was easier. He had his koosh ball, and I would frequently reach my hand down to touch him and remind him I was still there.

The first time I did this at our local grocery store almost got me arrested. As I was shopping, I noticed a man who seemed to be watching me. Not only was he watching, but he was following me through the store. After a bit, it got uncomfortable, and I hurriedly finished my shopping and left. Unbeknownst to me, he was the store's security guard. He had gone to the manager and told him I was shoplifting and putting things into the stroller I was pushing. The manager quickly pulled up the store video, saw me and started laughing. He then explained to the guard that I was a friend from church and told him all about Jacob.

That summer, our 15 year-old niece Tricia came down to visit. I told her all about Jacob and made sure she was forewarned. When she got there, she was not even bothered about his looks and became another of Jacob's fans. She told me I should have warned her about the deer mounts in the living room rather than Jacob since they upset her more than he did. It was nice to have her around to do things with Michelle and be another set of helping hands.

On one of our outings, I took the kids swimming at the pool and kept Jacob with me on the bleachers. Because of his g-tube, he couldn't be in chlorinated water. It wasn't long until one little girl came up to see Jacob. After looking for a bit, she said, "I don't like his face." I love the honesty of kids. I told her," He didn't get to pick out his face, he was just born with it." "Did you get to pick out your face?" She looked at me for a bit, then said, "No." She kept hanging around, and before long other kids came out of the water and joined her. When I looked up, I noticed that the only kids in the pool were mine. Finally, the lifeguard came over and told the kids to get back in the pool. Never heard a lifeguard say that before.

Kim was a control freak when it came to Jacob's benefits. She refused to have the Medicaid stickers sent to me; instead, she would send two each month. I had to ask her for more if I needed them. I got one for the doctor and one for the pharmacist. She also received Jacob's SSI check each month. He had been receiving $30.00 monthly while he was in the hospital. It should have gone up when he left, but Kim neglected to tell them about the change in his situation, so each month, we got $30.00. This money was specifically for Jacob's expenses like formula, diapers, clothes, etc. She would write me a check each month for $30.00 and demand receipts or the money returned. It was ridiculous since we bought everything he needed. The formula alone was more than $30.00 a month.

We also received a stipend from Community Connections. It was a hefty amount, so we didn't worry about spending money on Jacob. It is supposed to be for expenses that occurred in the course of caring for him, but we weren't in it for the money, so we didn't care. Jacob had everything he needed and that was what mattered. Money was never our motivation.

The first time Jacob pulled out his G-tube, I panicked and rushed him to the hospital. They popped one back in, and we headed home. I began to tape it to his stomach to give it a little more resistance and we were good for a bit. The second time, I went to pick him up out of his car seat, I heard that little pop and knew I'd done it again. We got back in the car and headed for the hospital. Since it had only been a couple of weeks since the last time, the ER doctor was a little miffed. He was also a little aggressive when he re-inserted it and then added a couple of stitches around the site so it wouldn't come out. When I got Jacob home and tried to feed him, the food wouldn't go in as it should, and he got really irritable the more I tried. I tried to draw some back out but only got digestive juices. I thought maybe it was because he'd pulled it out and had a new one put in, even though this hadn't happened the first time. When I tried to feed him the next morning, and it still wouldn't go in, I called a nurse friend and asked her what she thought. She said to try tugging on it a little to make sure it was against the stomach wall. I explained about the stitches, and she recommended a little Vaseline to make it slippery. It took about 20 minutes, but I could finally coax out 8" of tubing from his stomach. When I tried to feed him again, it went in fine. Apparently, the doctor had shoved it in so forcefully that it was right up against the opening to the intestines. I was unwittingly forcing food that wasn't broken down into his intestines. No wonder he was uncomfortable. This was the first time we experienced this lack of professionalism when people dealt with Jacob. Unfortunately, it wasn't the last.

Kim's visits were short and were mostly about gathering information. She would sometimes bring her mother, Claire, or her daughter. None of them interacted with Jacob, they just asked a bunch of questions and complained about everyone involved with his care. The daughter and Michelle were about the same age and got along well, so that was nice for her. They would spend the time playing and just being little girls.

Taking Jacob around town was always interesting. People had no idea how to respond and apparently never learned that old adage, "If you can't say something nice, don't say anything at all."

I did typing for the Pastor sometimes, and because Jacob was little, I would take him in with me. We were in the office one day where it was quiet. Jacob was sleeping in his stroller while I worked on the Pastor's sermon. People were decorating the church for an upcoming wedding. The family didn't attend our church, and so they hadn't encountered Jacob. As I was typing in the office, the mother of the bride came into the office to ask for something. The minute she saw Jacob, she stopped. Then she exclaimed loudly, "Oh my God, I thought that was a real baby!" Jacob was startled awake and began crying. As I went to pick him up, I told her gently that he was a real baby. She was mortified, turned, and left the building. I probably should have felt sorry for her, but this type of rudeness became so common that we just chalked it up to bad manners and moved on.

Some incidents were harder to ignore. In Ketchikan, each August, they have the annual Blueberry Festival downtown. Our church had a booth, and Michelle and I had made some blue popcorn balls with gummy worms in them for the booth. We headed into the hectic garage where the booths were set up. We had Jacob's blanket on his stroller, and Michelle was carrying the popcorn balls. When we got to the booth, it was so crowded I had a hard time maneuvering Jacob's stroller. There was a man nearby who caught a glimpse of Jacob and was desperately trying to get a better look. I tried to discretely turn the stroller away from him, but he started shoving people out of his way to get closer to the stroller. I told the ladies I needed to leave and started pushing my way out of the crowd. That's when I heard him yell for his kids to come and take a look at what he'd found. All the while still trying his best to get to Jacob. Michelle and I literally ran back to our vehicle to get away from him.

Another day while walking downtown, we encountered a couple. They were obviously tourists off the cruise ship and were probably really nice people. The woman saw the stroller and started to approach, saying, "Oh, a baby." I told her he was a special baby, but before I could finish, she replied, "Aren't they all" as she whipped off his blanket. The minute she saw him, she dropped the blanket and broke down. The poor husband kept apologizing as he led her away,

We met another couple while walking around Ward Lake. Dean had Jacob in a backpack carrier where he was enjoying the light and shadows made by the sun through the trees. As the couple approached, they began to talk to us and asked some non-intrusive and appropriate questions about Jacob. It was a refreshing change. It turned out he was a Shriner and ended up giving us contacts in case there was something the Shriners could do to help Jacob.

At the local taco place, we encountered a different reaction. When our waitress came over, she saw Jacob and panicked. She turned and hurried into the kitchen area. Eventually, the manager came over and apologized, then asked us to leave. He said the waitress was pregnant, and in her culture, Filipino, being around someone like Jacob would hurt her unborn baby. We were asked not to come back with Jacob.

There were those on the other side as well, just not as many. My friend Beth had recently had twin girls. When she brought them over to see Jacob, they both fell in love with him. They loved lying in our oversized bean bag and napping with him. They also named their dollies after him. I'm not sure how they really perceived him since they were about 18 months old, but they couldn't keep away. They caressed his face, held his hands, and just loved being around him.

There was also the Story Lady. This lady had a radio show where she read children's stories on air. Dean remembered her from his childhood. Somehow she heard about Jacob and wanted to do something for us. She decided to send us a case of diapers. When they arrived, we had no idea where they came from. We initially thought it might be from Kim, but when she denied it, we were stumped. We asked all our friends and finally found out. Although I never met her in person, I was extremely grateful for her kindness and the reminder that some people are just good.

Jacob began to respond more and more to the Disney movies he watched. He even began to hum the tunes as well as Twinkle Twinkle Little Star. When I told his doctor about it, he said I was imagining it. He thought I wanted Jacob to improve so much, I had tricked myself into believing it.

Jacob was finally able to hold up his head, and we were working on sitting. As time went on, others began to see development, and since he obviously wasn't dying, they began to discuss his future.

Doctor J ordered a head CT scan on Jacob to see if anything had changed since his shunt had been inserted. He was surprised to see that his brain had grown to fill the space of the fluid. He still cautioned us not to expect too much since the brain was still abnormal.

As Jacob developed, they had to address the question of what should be done to give him optimum life, rather than keeping him comfortable until he died. They finally came up with a long-term plan that started with correcting his clubbed feed to enable him to wear shoes and, hopefully, one day, walk. There were also concerns regarding his vision, hearing, nutritional needs, and occupational therapy issues. A plan was made to take him to Children's Hospital in Seattle for evaluation.

Out of the blue, Kim called and asked us to consider adopting Jacob. We were completely taken off guard. We talked about it for several days and ran through every scenario we could think of. We prayed about it and got counsel from our pastor. In the end, we decided it wasn't the right choice for us. When we told Kim, she accepted our decision so nonchalantly that it was almost like she'd forgotten that she had asked. Had we known the future, we would have taken the risk and made a different choice.

The deformity of Jacob's mouth made speech difficult, but he was able to make sounds using his tongue and his fist. His favorites were la-la-la and da. Dean decided it was time for Jacob to say Dada. He worked with him for over an hour, coaxing and praising him until it happened. "Dada" was Jacob's first word. It wasn't long until Michelle and I were wishing he'd never learned to say Dada. It was all we heard for the next few days. Dean, of course, thought it was awesome and kept encouraging him.

Jacob couldn't make the "mmm" sound so we worked on signing Mom. It took some time but we got there in the end.

There were many phone calls and discussions about comfort versus function. The doctors were reluctant to make decisions about expensive and potentially dangerous surgeries if Jacob wasn't going to truly benefit from them. It was decided that no decisions would be made until they got the results back from Children's Hospital.

I naturally assumed Kim would take him to Seattle, which caused me a little concern since she had never been his caregiver and knew nothing about him as a person, only the medical side. As the plans progressed, she told me she wanted me to take him. I was really surprised. Then she told me she was pregnant and wasn't up to the trip.

Michelle and I took Jacob to Seattle. Since this was his first flight, I wasn't sure how he would react to the change in pressure. I was pleased that he did great and even slept for part of the flight. When we got to Seattle, we drove to Kid's Village, a temporary residence next to Children's Hospital, where families of patients can stay. Even here, Jacob was something of a spectacle, but everyone was nice and made us feel at ease. Our day at the hospital was grueling. I'm pretty sure we were seen by every clinic in the place. He was screened and evaluated by Ophthalmology, Audiology, Nutrition, Orthopedics, Orthotics, Speech and Language, Craniofacial, Physical Therapy, Dental, Gastroenterology, Genetics, Neurodevelopmental, Occupational Therapy, and Oral and Maxillofacial surgery. It was exhausting for all of us. Jacob suffered from <u>white coat syndrome</u> and a day full of being poked and prodded made him irritable and uncooperative.

When I got home, I passed on everything I could remember to Kim and Dr. J. When the reports finally came in, the decision was made to operate on his clubbed feet and repair his hernia. They also began working up plans for further corrective surgeries.

Before Jacob left us, I wanted to get a family picture. I didn't know what the future held or if I would ever see him again, and he was definitely part of our family by now. Dean had an old friend who did photography. He called him and explained our situation. Norm agreed to do our photos. When we got there, he was a little shocked, but he did a great job and I now had pictures of all of us together.

Kim decided that following Jacob's surgery, he needed to be in the Seattle area, where his doctors would have easier access to him.

The plan was to start working towards corrective surgery, and there would be lots of appointments. She found a children's home that would take him rather than placing him in another foster home.

Dean and I visited Ashley House, the home Kim arranged to have Jacob placed in when he was released from the hospital. We got a tour and met several residents and staff. There was an infant who couldn't control his body temperature, so he was left in a crib in a temperature-controlled room. Another little girl was anencephalic and did nothing. A young man had drowned as a child and was revived. His brain damage was so severe he required 24-hour care. There wasn't anyone here like Jacob. Jacob hummed his favorite songs, laughed when tickled, and loved to play and romp. It broke my heart to think of him here in this home where children came to die. I knew he wouldn't understand where we were and why no one played with him. I was afraid he would just give up. When we left, we were very sad to think of our happy little boy in this home. Ashley House was a beautiful home filled with caring staff, but the children here were severely impaired. Jacob's happy, playful personality just didn't fit. This home was medicinal, quiet and so very sad. The children there were not interactive and playful: they were like vacant shells which were simply being tended to. We went home with heavy hearts.

The last month we had Jacob, SSI finally upped his monthly check to $400.00. Kim sent it over with a note insisting that all $400.00 be spent on Jacob, and anything left over had to be returned to her along with receipts. It was so insulting. We had paid for everything this child needed and lots he didn't for the last eight months and never once complained or asked her for anything. Yet she acted like we were somehow trying to take advantage of her and Jacob. I took Jacob shopping and bought him $500.00 worth of outfits, PJs, socks, toys, and anything else I could find. And yes, I sent her the receipts.

Shortly before Jacob left, we learned that along with his SSI check, Medicaid also sent eight months of reimbursement for all the months he wasn't getting the full amount. Kim kept that for herself. She said she thought it was for her expenses.

A few weeks later, I flew to Washington with Jacob. We spent the night with a dear friend, and she drove us to the hospital the next morning. Kim met us at the hospital, and we got Jacob all checked in and ready for surgery. After surgery, I accompanied Kim to see Jacob. He was pretty out of it, but the doctor said the surgery had gone pretty well. They found some unusual things during the operation. Apparently, Jacob had two <u>vas deferens</u> and some missing bones in his feet. They did the best they could and cast both feet. After the casts came off, he would be fitted with <u>Ankle-Foot Orthoses,</u> or AFO's for short, for support. The hope was that he would eventually be able to walk. I was glad I was able to see him and give him a kiss before I left. Kim asked me to accompany her to the nurse's desk. She told them who I was and asked them to put in his chart that I could get updates on Jacob if I called in. I thanked her, said my goodbyes, and headed to the airport.

The next morning I called Children's to see how he was doing. I was told that after I left, Kim returned to the nurse's station and told them that I was not to receive any information about Jacob and I was not permitted to see him. She said that he was very needy right now, and she wanted him to need her.

One of the things that happened when Jacob left was the adjustment back to "normal life." It was a roller coaster of emotions. On one hand, it was so easy to live my daily life. No longer were we invaded by Jacob's people. Outings were a breeze, and the stress level fell tremendously. I, however, felt terrible guilt for enjoying the ease of my life. I also felt like I had let Jacob down, and I worried about him. I hoped he was being loved and cared for. The Aunties became even dearer to us after Jacob left. They were super supportive as we re-adjusted to life without him.

When Jacob was discharged, he went to Ashley House. One of the nurses at Ashley House fell in love with him. She recognized that Jacob did not need to be in that type of setting; he needed a home and a family to love him. She spent time interacting with him and eventually got Kim to agree to her taking Jacob home to live with her family. I don't know how she got Kim to agree, but I was so glad she did. I imagine that her being a nurse probably helped.

1990

When Jacob went to live with V and S, she sent me a letter with some pictures. I was so excited to get an update on our boy. V told me she had received Jacob's scrapbook and was already adding things to it. She and S were such a great fit for Jacob, and he was thriving. I received the following letter from her about three months after I last saw Jacob.

Dearest McFarland's

This is a long-overdue update on Jacob. I'm sorry for the delay – I'm not much at letter writing for some reason.

Jacob saw the medical team at Children's on the 12th. They were all very skeptical at first, but once Jacob patty caked, they were convinced that this precious little lad does indeed have intelligence. The docs had tears as they observed Jacob's bag of tricks and S and I were laughing and crying simultaneously as it sunk in that they had been impressed enough to go the whole 9 yards with Jacob!

The neurosurgeon is hoping to start soon on cranial surgery to prevent further crowding of the brain. He will start at the base of the skull, and because this involves the spinal cord, Jacob will be in a holo-traction for many weeks. (This is a metal frame attached to screws in the skull and secured to a harness-type frame over the shoulders).

Either S or I plan to be with Jacob during his entire hospital stay. For our own piece of mind as well as his.

Vision screening under EEG shows Jacob has fairly normal vision!

The final leg cast came off 2/15, and Jacob has a beautiful new foot. He will sleep in splints until he's walking. We went to Toys R Us afterward. Jacob got some more new toys (more challenging toys!) and new shoes.

With a cone of rings, Jacob can quickly remove all the rings but so far refuses to put them back. We notice he's quite possessive, so he probably thinks we're taking the rings away from him when we put them back on the cone! Character! We want you to always feel good about the little boy you gave so much. Love is never wasted, and the love and security you gave Jacob has helped him to be strong for all he has ahead.

Presently Jacob is teething big time! His upper teeth are giving him a hard time. Because he can't chew, we spend a lot of time massaging his gums. He has four teeth trying to erupt at once. The two front teeth and two molars. The orthodontist says they are coming in at the correct position! He was started on fluoride. Strong teeth are essential because they will be used to wire his jaws into place. So evidently, there will be nothing done to his mouth until his teeth are in. We love Jacob so much. He's been such a blessing. It amazes us one little boy can give so much joy. Everyone he touches feels it. We don't know what the future holds, but for now, Jacob is loved and secure again. And we will make every effort to see that maintained. Take care of yourselves. You're wonderful and you've given more than you'll ever realize.

Gratefully V

P.S. This is to be our first and last correspondence because the family requests all exchanges of info be through them. I'm sorry

Not long after, I received the following letter from Kim.

Hello Dean and Kelly

I have been trying to reach you since the end of May, but each time I called, no one answered, and now the number's been disconnected.

I'm sure you're wondering how Jacob is doing. He's great.

He has started to bear weight on his feet and legs. He rolls all over too. His strength is building in his arms, neck, back and legs of course.

They scheduled him for surgery to reshape the skull but it has been canceled three times due to post-nasal drip - yep - his nasal passages are there somewhere.

He is thriving & S & V are so good to & for him. The State of WA & the social workers there have been a real blessing - AK hasn't scoffed since they agreed on his placement.

Jacob weighs around 25# now & is 29". He looks good. He says Mama by sticking his hand in his mouth as well as bye-bye.

He is undergoing physical therapy regularly & now the therapist has said she feels Jacob has made so many gains that he would benefit from a more in-depth program like a school of sorts.

I appreciated the gifts for Zachary, Kelly. Thank you a lot. I wanted to say thanks for all you've done for Jacob too. If you get south & have a chance to visit Jacob - I'm sure you could make arrangements with S & V to see him.

I don't mean to keep you away or in the dark about Jacob. I intended to tell you a date for surgery, too, but none is set to date.

I must apologize for all that has happened with your family and Jacob - but I'm sure you'll agree that Jacob is far better off away from the Ketchikan general scene.

If you want & do get a chance to see him, I'm quite sure you'll be amazed at his progress.

I hope you are all well

Take care,

I will let you know the surgery date if you are interested.

God bless your family

Sincerely, Kim

After Jacob left, we continued to do foster care. Some of the kids were pretty easy to care for, and others were a mess. The abuse and neglect we saw was unbelievable. I don't know how much good we did them, but at least they had a safe home for a while.

In the summer of 1990, we got an unexpected phone call from our pastor. He heard about a pregnant young woman who wanted to give her baby up for adoption. He wanted to know if we were interested. We definitely were!

Heather was in jail for a mandatory three days because of a DWI. While she was incarcerated, she told the guard that she was pregnant and had received no prenatal care. After he made arrangements for her to see the doctor, she told him she wanted to give the child up for adoption. She asked if he knew anyone who was interested. Dan, another friend from our church, contacted our pastor. Before we knew it, we had a date to meet Heather.

She was living in a run-down apartment building called the Knickerbocker Hotel. We were a little concerned when we got there and saw how sketchy it was. We made our way upstairs and knocked on her door. Heather let us into a dark room lit only by the windows. A little girl was playing on the floor, and various people were asleep around the room. Heather was a petite blonde who did not look pregnant at all. She introduced us to her three-year-old daughter Mindy and told us about herself.

She was married to a young man whom Dean remembered from his childhood. She and her husband were separated and getting a divorce. She was currently working at a downtown bar where she met Kurt. He was with a band from California. He was the father of the baby. She called him when she found out she was pregnant, and he had no interest in the baby. As she was on her own and already had one child to care for, she felt that giving him up for adoption would be best for everyone. She was five months pregnant.

We talked for a bit and told her about ourselves. We told her we'd love to adopt her baby.

Michelle was super excited. We'd been praying for a little brother or sister for years, and now it was finally happening. Not only would she have a sibling, but it would be a newborn with no baggage.

The wait began. Heather would call me with updates, and eventually, she agreed that I could be there when she delivered. She also had an HIV test done because, as she said, she didn't know what her ex had been up to and just wanted to be sure.

Michelle and I were excitedly getting the house ready for another baby. When Heather had an ultrasound, they told her the baby's sex, but she decided she didn't want us to know. She wanted it to be a surprise.

As fall arrived, we were busy building a huge maze inside our church for the annual harvest party. Dean and I had so much fun with all the different things we built into our fun house. There was Jonah in the belly of the whale, a jello pool, talking hands and all kinds of other silly things. All this kept us occupied as we waited for our new addition.

Michelle had decided that her costume would be an autumn tree with real maple leaves. She went next door and asked the neighbors if it was okay if she collected some fallen leaves from their yard. They gave her permission, and she went about collecting them. I was still at the house, but after a bit, I thought I heard something and went outside to see if she was calling me. I didn't hear anything and was just about to head back inside when I saw her coming around the corner. She was covered in mud and was accompanied by another neighbor and his full-size poodle named Teddy. As she got closer, I could see she was crying, and I rushed to her. The neighbor explained that he had just gotten home from the night shift and heard her scream as he got out of his car. He and Teddy rushed down his driveway, and then he saw her. There were two dogs on her - one at her throat and one at her groin. Teddy chased them off, and our neighbor helped her up and brought her home. He didn't know how badly she was hurt, but there didn't seem to be any blood. I thanked him and took her inside.

She was still sobbing and couldn't tell me what was hurting. Since she was covered in mud, I took her into the shower with me and started to take off her muddy things so I could see where she was hurt. That's when she started screaming that she couldn't see. She became hysterical, and it was an ordeal to get her cleaned up and out of the shower. When I examined her, I couldn't find any puncture wounds or bites, but she was still hysterical.

I called Dean at work and told him what had happened and that I was taking her to the doctor. She calmed down a bit by the time we got to the doctor's office. He examined her, and because it was an animal attack, he called animal control. Although there were no puncture wounds, the pressure of the dog bites scarred Michelle through her clothing and coat. If she hadn't had her coat on, it could have been much worse. After we filled out all the paperwork and answered all their questions, we came home. Michelle was feeling better and still wanted to attend the harvest party.

I updated Dean on Michelle and all the paperwork and questioning from animal control. We knew who owned the dogs, and we told them. Dean worked with the guy who lived in the lower house, and he promised Dean that they would do anything they could to help. He also assured Dean the dogs would be put down. However, when animal control went to get the animals, the wife refused to relinquish them and denied that it was her dogs that had attacked Michelle. There wasn't any doubt as the neighbor saw them, and we all knew who they belonged to. They were always running around the neighborhood. The troopers had to be called in before she would let them take the dogs away.

When we got home from the party, we got a call from the wife. She acted like she wasn't sure what had happened but had heard that our daughter might have been attacked. I told her exactly what happened, and she was very apologetic and even told me her son had scars from a dog attack when he was younger. That made the whole situation even weirder. I would have expected her to act differently since she'd been through it herself.

The next day we got a call from animal control. The owner had petitioned to have the animals sent to a logging camp in an isolated area rather than having them destroyed. I was furious. She maintained that her dogs were not dangerous and that she didn't believe it had even been them that attacked Michelle. We were told this could turn into a long, drawn-out battle. Michelle reacted badly. She was terrified. She wouldn't go outside without one of us with her.

I wanted to assure her that the dogs couldn't hurt her. So I took her to the pound so she could see that they were in cages. After we got permission, we walked back toward the cages they were in. They were completely calm until they saw her, then they went ballistic, snarling, barking, and trying to get at her. She freaked out and literally tried to crawl up the side of me to get away from them. I felt horrible. All I wanted to do was reassure her, and instead, I re-traumatized her. That night Dean talked to the husband and asked him what was going on. Apparently, he had no idea what his wife was up to and thought the dogs had already been euthanized. He apologized and promised they would be put down immediately.

Michelle was a mess. She was afraid of everything. She wouldn't go outside by herself. She wouldn't talk to people she didn't know. She became withdrawn and quiet. And she was terrified of dogs - all dogs except Teddy, her hero.

We expected that over time Michelle, our precocious child, would return, but it didn't happen. She allowed her fear to change her, and nothing we did helped.

As I look back, I think what Michelle really experienced that day was a loss of innocence. Only it wasn't lost over time as God intended, but ripped violently from her in that moment. For the first time in her life she realized she was vulnerable. Every situation in her life was being re-evaluated and she saw risk and danger everywhere she looked. As a victim of abuse I understood her fears but didn't know how to help her get beyond them. I was broken-hearted as I watched her pull more and more insider herself.

Finally, Heather's due date arrived. Heather and I were in regular communication, and after one false alarm, we were both anxious about the arrival. One day I called to check on her and was told she was gone. No one knew where she went or what her plans were. We had to assume she'd changed her mind even though she had never intimated that she had doubts. We didn't know what to think. For the next week, we just kind of walked around in a fog, waiting and hoping.

We got a call a week later that she was in labor. She told us she was in Oregon and that the baby was coming. I asked her if it was a boy or a girl, and she told me it was a boy. Later she called back and told us our boy was born, and he was 7# 19".

The next day I flew down to get our baby. I was tired from all the hectic planning of the night before and anxious about everything in front of me. I was met at the airport by Heather's aunt and uncle. Heather was staying with them, along with her mother and brother. When I got to the house, I was shown to Heather's room. There she was in bed with Mindy and our baby boy. He was all swollen and puffy. His nose was bruised, but he looked perfect to me. She handed him to me, and I was done.

Heather told me about leaving on the ferry to come to see her mom, who was dying of cancer. Even though she was past her due date, she was able to hide her belly under a big flannel shirt. After she had been there a couple of days, her aunt took her in to see her OB/GYN. He found her dilated to 10 and fully effaced. She had a contraction in the doctor's office, and he sent her to the hospital. After being admitted, she was allowed to shower, during which time the baby literally fell through the birth canal and was delivered in the shower by her aunt. This explained a lot about the bruising. The doctor missed the entire birth but billed us for his services nonetheless.

Because our baby was born in Oregon, we ran into legal issues with the Interstate Compact, which affects the adoption of Oregon children being adopted in other states. Apparently, Heather was told about it while she was in the hospital. She contacted a lawyer who said I could not take the baby out of the state until it was dealt with. All this forced me to hire an Oregon lawyer, as my Ketchikan lawyer couldn't help me with it. He felt pretty sure it shouldn't apply since Heather was only visiting. Nonetheless, I had to hire an attorney in Oregon to get it settled. This also meant I had to stay in Oregon longer than I anticipated. Heather's aunt and uncle graciously offered to have me stay with them as long as I needed to.

I slept with Baby Boy in bed with me since there was no crib, and I was surprised that he wouldn't settle down and sleep. He was agitated, and the more I tried to comfort him, the more agitated he got. I eventually laid him completely apart from me. I placed pillows all around him and he finally went to sleep. It wasn't a big deal, but something didn't feel quite right about it.The next three days were spent on the phone with lawyers, the hospital, and the doctor. The state of Oregon was trying to apply the Interstate Compact to our situation even though Heather wasn't an Oregon resident. We eventually got it straightened out with three lawyers, three days, and lots of money.

I got to know Heather's family, and we took lots of pictures of Baby Boy with all the family members. Her brother was nice, but Connie, her mom, was antagonistic toward me. She made sure I knew she was not in favor of me adopting Baby Boy and that she would take him herself if she wasn't so sick. However, before we left, she did finally give me her approval. She said if he had to be adopted by someone, she was glad it was me. Connie died the following summer.

When I finally got the all-clear, we caught a plane to Portland. The flight was magical. I sat in my seat with Baby Boy in his snugglie and watched lightning light up the night sky. I held his hand, caressed his head, felt his heartbeat, and immersed myself in his newborn baby smell. After I had been told I couldn't have any more children, God spoke to my heart and assured me that I would have a son. I knew we still had to settle all the legal and financial matters, but I finally had my son.

When we got to Portland, we were snowed in and did not know when we could get out. I called Dean to let him know we had another delay. Then I called Uncle Vince and Aunt Judy, and they graciously drove to Portland and took us home with them. We ended up staying with them for two days before the weather cleared up enough for us to get home. By the time we left, Aunt Judy had fallen in love with "Wee Baby Boy," and Little Grandma was convinced that her newest great-grandson had smiled at her. I loved being with them and so appreciated their hospitality, but I wanted to get home and introduce Baby Boy to the rest of his family.

We finally made it home five days later. Dean and Michelle were so excited to have us home. Unfortunately, the excitement wore off pretty quickly for Michelle.

We had re-outfitted the crib for the baby, and Michelle was seriously offended. Even though her crib had been used for Jacob and other babies we cared for, she didn't want him in her bed. I went into the room and found the bedclothes on the floor with eight-year-old Michelle asleep in her crib. It wasn't long before she started asking us to send him back.

Baby Boy continued to be distant, and I was beginning to be concerned. He would not be comforted by close contact or snuggling. He would not be held in a horizontal position, always upright and with as little contact as possible. I admit to being disappointed as I am very tactile, and it felt like rejection. I talked to other adoptive parents and started hearing about attachment disorders.

Another odd thing I noticed was his smell. He had a distinctive body odor that wasn't bad, just different. Years later, after talking to other adoptive parents, I found out that most of them had to get used to this "different" smell their children had as well.

Heather came out to the house after she returned from Oregon to see us. She brought a letter she'd written to Baby Boy and spent time asking about him but didn't want to hold him. I figured that was her way of letting go.

1991

Our court date finally arrived in January. At court, we ran into Heather with her ex. Apparently, they were back together. We went before the judge with the adoption and name change petition. Heather told the judge that she had spoken to the birth father, and he had no interest in the child. The judge said something to us during all the legalities that really had an impact on me. He said that we needed to be sure of our decision because once it was final, it would be easier to give up our daughter than to un-adopt the baby. Once it was over, we had our son. Baby Boy was now Keagan, and he was all ours.

After the adoption, we kept in contact with Heather just so she could know he was okay. I would let her know how he was doing and send her pictures occasionally. We never tried to hide the fact that Keagan was adopted; it was just part of who he was.

As Keagan continued to shy away from touch, Dr. J and I discussed my concerns. He felt like FAS/FAE was more likely than attachment disorders. He ran some tests and said everything looked fine, but we really wouldn't be able to see any type of learning disabilities until he was older.

When Keagan was around nine months he started having difficulty breathing. The doctor put him on steroids and a nebulizer. He threw up the steroids and the nebulizer was a 10-minute scream fest. He fought every treatment. Still not sure if it was the medication or being confined for 10 minutes that he hated more. He was finally diagnosed with infant asthma, and we were sent to Seattle for allergy tests. The only allergen he reacted to was the test one. We were told that he was what they called a "happy wheezer" because he had large bronchial tubes. So even though he sounded like a freight train, he was getting oxygen. We were also told that even though his lungs showed damage and he would likely suffer from respiratory ailments his entire life, he could outgrow asthma. Thank God that is exactly what happened. By the time he reached two and a half, he had no more asthma. To this day, he hasn't had anything more serious than the flu.

We continued to take foster kids as the need arose. Most of these were short-term or emergency placements. Because Keagan was so young, we weren't interested in taking on a child long-term.

Keagan remained physically distant, but we began to see another side as well. He was hyper-vigilant and would often react to simple things with massively violent over-reactions. At two, he threatened to have the dog rip his dad's throat out when he didn't get his way. He looked perfectly angelic, but the blonde hair blue eyed boy was a raging volcano just waiting to erupt.

There were even weirder things. One day we were heading to the fruit stand at Wolf Point. Fresh fruit is a total luxury on the Alaskan island, and when it comes in on the ferry, there is a rush to buy it. When we got there, however, Keagan crawled under the dash and refused to get out of the vehicle. When I asked him what was wrong, he pointed out the window and said, "That's a bad woman. I hate that woman." When I looked outside, I saw Heather, his birth mother. We hadn't seen her in over a year, and I knew he didn't know who she was, but he was adamant about wanting nothing to do with her. When I finally pried him out from under the dash, he hid behind me. When Heather saw us, she came over to say hi. We spoke, but when she bent down to say hi to Keagan, he hid behind me and would have nothing to do with her.

Keagan had a hard time with anyone laughing at him. Even if he did something adorably cute, we weren't allowed to laugh, or he would get really mad. When he was two, he was telling me about the picture he'd colored in Nursery. He pronounced it "He-ho-ho-i-mus." When I laughed, he was so offended he wouldn't even try to say it again until he'd mastered the word hippopotamus.

He would frequently get really angry, and usually, it was directed at me. It was like he was just waiting for something to tick him off, and then he felt justified to respond. Dean and I were completely at a loss to understand what was going on with our little man.

1992

Jacob was gone for about three years when, out of the blue, we got a phone call from Kim. She told us she was moving Jacob back to Alaska and wanted to know if we would take him back. We talked about it and agreed. When we decided to take Jacob back, we didn't have long discussions or weigh the pros and cons. We just said, "Yes." We knew we'd be giving up our quiet normal lives as we took on Jacob's people again, but it didn't matter. Jacob was family, and when family needs you, you do whatever you can to help.

Kim gave us an update on Jacob's life. She told us Jacob had undergone craniofacial surgery. The surgery took 18 hours, and he lost 7x his body's blood volume. His good eye had been damaged, and the surgeons had not been able to accomplish all they set out to do. What they had accomplished was to replace the floating cartilage of his forehead with skull bone, split and pieced together with screws and plates. They brought his palate down and gathered skin that would be used to build him a nose at a later date. All in all, she said, it was a good first step to reconstructing his face.

Jacob was now living with a wonderful foster mom, according to Kim, near Children's Hospital. We were given strict instructions not to contact V & S.

I immediately contacted V to find out what had happened. She filled me in on what led up to the surgery and what followed. Kim played the same game she had with us. After surgery, she refused to let them visit Jacob or get any updates regarding his recovery. She completely shut them out with no explanation except her go-to, "He's very needy right now, and I want him to need me." It still amazes me how little thought she gave to what Jacob needed. He had just been through a horrific ordeal and had no way to communicate his needs. Then he woke up to a stranger who wanted him to somehow make her feel better about her own life while giving him nothing in return. Kim never understood why others were so drawn to him. She could see how much joy he gave others, and she wanted that for herself. She just kept going about it in all the wrong ways, and Jacob had to suffer for it. Once again, he was deserted by his family. V and S were devastated about losing him but were relieved that at least he was coming back here where he would be loved and cared for.

After Jacob was released from the hospital, Kim had him placed in a foster home in the Seattle area so he would be near his doctors. He was also enrolled in school, and Kim didn't want me to move him before school was out.

Michelle and I flew to Seattle to see Jacob, talk to his doctor and make arrangements to move him back home. When I contacted the foster mother, she said it wasn't convenient for me to come to her house. Instead, she requested that I visit Jacob at his school. At this point, I had not seen Jacob since he left us, with the exception of pictures V sent despite Kim's mandate. The last ones I saw looked like our little boy. When I saw him at school, I was shocked. The surgery made him look more abnormal than before, as far as I was concerned. But what really upset me was his general appearance. He was overweight and dirty, his hair was long and stringy, and he was just generally unkempt. He was wearing a girl's purple sweat-suit that was too big for him. I was angry because I knew that V and S had spoiled Jacob, and he had a better wardrobe than most women. Why did he look like this? Why wasn't he at least clean? Once I started to interact with him and saw he was still my Jake-O-Bean, all I wanted to do was take him home.

I went to see Jacob's surgeon. I wanted to know what was being planned and what concerns they had. And, what was next? We talked about what they'd like to do and how difficult it had been working with the parents. He told me that some doctors were now refusing to see Jacob because of the threats issued by his parents.

The next planned procedure would be to insert a balloon under Jacob's facial skin, which would be injected with saline slowly over time. This would stretch the skin so they'd then be able to construct a nose to give him a more normal appearance.

I went home and began to prepare for Jacobs' homecoming. I had been teaching preschool and art classes at KCA, where Michelle was again attending. Keagan was taken care of in the Nursery with his friend Toshie. I had to resign because there was no way I could continue to teach and take care of Jacob. His situation was too involved and would once again take up most of my time.

JoAnna was again in our lives. As she got all the legal and financial aspects worked out with Kim and George, we found out more information. The parents were now divorced. Kim had sole custody of the other three children, but they had joint custody of

Jacob. So every decision had to be approved by both of them. Hopefully, this wouldn't be problematic.

Keagan was super excited to be getting a brother. Michelle, although excited about Jacob, wasn't really thrilled about all the attention he drew. She was a pre-teen now, and appearances were everything. She was also not the same girl she had been. Following the attack, she remained withdrawn to a degree, and we didn't know how she was going to handle all the changes. I didn't know how the family dynamic would work, but we did what we could to prepare everyone.

I also let the Aunties know Jacob was coming home. G and C were excited to see him again. G taught the Special Needs Preschool class, and C was the school's Occupational Therapist, so they would be with him at school. That alone made the transition so much easier.

Michelle and I went to Seattle to get Jacob. There were a couple of doctor appointments to attend to and get his things together. We went to his foster home and were disgusted by what we saw. The reason I was given for not being able to see Jacob at the foster home when I visited previously was that the foster mom was preparing to go to Japan. She would be speaking on fostering children with special needs, as she was the darling of the Seattle agency. What I saw made me sick to my stomach. Jacob was no longer being fed by his g-tube but had been fitted with a <u>j-tube</u>. I was told this was because he was throwing up. J-tube feedings require a pump that slowly pumps the formula directly into the intestines. Since it isn't broken down in the stomach, it has to be delivered in small increments. I imagine after the trauma of surgery, he probably needed that, but by now, he should be back on his g-tube or even oral feedings. V had him drinking out of a cup before surgery, and now that his upper palate was re-aligned, it should have been even easier.

As it was, when Jacob came home from school, he was put to bed, put on his pump, and left until time for school the next day. This accounted for his weight gain. His bed was a crib with no sheets or blankets at all. The foster mom said it was because he took them off. His roommate was a twelve-year-old severely disabled girl who lay in her crib all day as well.

The morning I picked up Jacob to spend the day with us, I saw a helper giving his roommate a bath. When I brought him back that evening, she was still lying on the towel in the bed, completely naked, except for her diaper. I couldn't wait to get Jacob out of there. There were other children in the home as well, but since I was led in to get Jacob and led out again, I couldn't get a sense of what their situations were. I was told she had six children in her care.

We got Jacob's things and brought him back to Kid's Village with us. We then went shopping for new clothes, a car seat and shoes. When we got back, we tossed everything she sent and gave Jacob a bath. After a haircut, he started looking more like the old Jacob. I know he was showered with nice clothes and tons of toys while with V and S, but none of that made it back to me. I don't know where it went, but I can guess. I was just happy that his baby book survived. I then fed him with his <u>Mic-key button</u> (a button that replaces the g-tube in older children), which was still in place, and he threw up the whole amount. The next feeding, I went slower, and he did fine. I never did use the j-tube and pump.

When we got home, all the visits, phone calls and doctor appointments started up again. Life was once again very hectic. Two distinct differences were Michelle and Keagan. Michelle was now very aware of the reactions of people around us and the comments being made. She would often want to stay in the car or stay home rather than go with the family. Keagan surprisingly took to Jacob immediately, and they became best buds.

As Jacob was now back on gastrointestinal feedings and re-learning to drink by mouth, his excess weight fell off, and he was back to his old self in no time.

With Medicaid, special formulas and diapers are paid for once the child reaches the age of three. Jacob's supplies; Pediasure, diapers, wipes, syringes, tubes, swabs, and replacement Mic-Keys were all covered. These supplies were sent to the home each month. When Jacob got home, we received our first shipment and were so surprised. He received six cans of Pediasure per/day (he only drank 3), ten diapers per day (he only used 4), as well as ten depends per day. The foster mom said she ordered these because he was flooding the diapers, so she used both on him. I never saw him with one of these on. In fact, all his supplies were way in excess. I contacted the supply company and told them there had been a mistake. They assured me this was his regular order. I can only assume she was using his supplies for other foster children that weren't covered by Medicaid. I contacted Medicaid and told them what I suspected and was told to mind my own business.

Kim was even more antagonistic than before. She had nothing nice to say about most of the doctors at the Children's Hospital and made a lot of threats. She began to call Jacob her million-dollar baby because that's what she was going to get when she sued everyone she was mad at. I began to see why so many of the doctors would no longer work with Jacob. It was really unfortunate because, in the end, Jacob was the one who suffered. I also felt that it was in our best interest if I started keeping a journal of incidents, phone calls, appointments, meetings, and anything else that might be used against us. It was just for me, but I really felt like I should start documenting things.

Before Jacob left us, he had begun to say Da-Da with his fist in his mouth. Because of his palate, speaking was not easy, but V and S told us he had learned to say several words while in Washington. He was also signing several words, but after surgery, he lost it all. We were excited to see if he could re-learn speech. Unfortunately, he did not, but he did start to sign a few words again. It warmed my heart when he looked at me and signed, "Mom."

Michelle had a hard time when Jacob returned. It wasn't that she didn't love Jacob and was glad he was back, but she was a pre-teen, and what her friends thought of her was important. The first time Jacob was with us, Michelle had been his biggest advocate. She even punched a boy at school for saying her brother was ugly. But now, she didn't want the attention he brought. She didn't like all the drama around the house. It was a rough adjustment. Keagan, on the other hand, was thrilled. He finally had a brother he could play with. Jacob and Keagan adored each other. They were around the same size, although two years apart, and Keagan loved all the new stuff Jacob brought.

One of my favorite pictures is of the boys on the porch on Jacob's first day of school. Jacob is handsome in his jeans and jacket, with his hair combed back, standing with his mini-man walker. Keagan is beside him in his matching denims and they are both smiling. Because they were the same size, I got to play a bit and dress them similarly. One day at the store, a lady stopped me with the comment, "Oh, how cute, are they twins?" I wanted to say, oh yes, identical, but I couldn't be that mean.

Keagan and Jacob shared a bedroom with twin beds. One day we heard a ruckus and went back to see what was going on. Keagan was jumping on his bed while Jake was sitting and bouncing up and down. I told Keagan to stop jumping and for Jacob to get back on his own bed. Then we had to stand there and wait while Jacob climbed down, across the divide, and up onto his bed. When he finally made it, we scolded them both and put them back to bed. I wasn't sure I would be able to hold in the laughter until we got back to the living room. Those two were so precious together.

We got a swing set and put it on the deck. The boys would spend hours out there going up and down the slide and swinging. Of course, I had to go out and put Jacob on the slide and hold him on the swing, but they had so much fun on it. When the weather was nice, I would fill a kiddie pool and put it at the bottom of the slide. Jacob would hang out in the water while Keagan went up and down.

Once we all got settled, we began to make plans for Jacob to go to school. Auntie G was going to be his teacher, and we were thrilled. She was a little concerned about the other parent's reaction to Jacob, so she organized an informational meeting with them. She invited the parents and told them all about Jacob. She showed them pictures and answered all their questions. We felt we were ready for the first day of school.

The first morning of school, Jacob was in the classroom with G when one little girl, whose parents had been out of town at the time of the meeting, walked in. She took one look at Jacob and strutted up to Auntie G's desk. She demanded, "Where's my mask? He's got a mask, where's my mask?" Auntie G calmly replied that he didn't have a mask that was his face. She looked Jacob over again and said, "Oh, okay." The kids in his class quickly came to love Jacob. He was so happy and funny, and they loved hanging out with him and pushing him around in his chair. Once he started school, I couldn't go anywhere in town without someone stopping me to tell me how they knew Jacob and that he was their friend.

Jacob was now mobile and much harder to ignore. The minute he heard a male voice, he would make a beeline toward them and hold out his hands to be picked up. This could be a little startling when people weren't expecting him.

Papa was great. He'd always pick him up and tell him he was a good boy. Jacob loved sitting in Papa's lap because he always had interesting things in his pockets that Jacob could find.

Jacob had a thing for paper, and we frequently gave him a magazine to look at. Because of his vision issues, he saw best at about 3". Because of his right eye's unusual attachment, he would use his hand to pull his eyelid up, which enabled him to see better.

When he was given a magazine, he'd remove all the little cards from inside, then go back and scan every single page. Then he'd shred it and move on to the next one. Papa gave him one of his photography magazines, and oddly enough, Jacob didn't shred it but kept it for quite a long time. We later realized it was the one that showed techniques for filming models at the beach, and we started calling it his girlie magazine. Jacob loved it and would take it with him when we went in the car and on the bus. One day he came home from school without his girlie magazine, but rather a Cabela's catalog. He was not impressed.

Another time I went into the living room to check on Jacob and found him beside the bookcase with every book he could reach pulled off the shelf and piled around him. He had Dean's Bible and was crinkling and tearing the pages out. I think he liked the way they sounded when he wadded them up. He got scolded and told to go to his room. He was the slowest child, hence the nickname Sloth man, and it took him forever to crawl down the hallway. The funny thing was that he sounded like he was running because he would pound his hands as he slowly made his way.

Jacob loved music. V told me about one of his favorites, "Bushel and A Peck." I'd never heard of it, but I looked it up, and when I sang it to Jacob, he recognized it and was so happy. He would rock back and forth, clap his hands, and hum along with me. It became our night time song. There was another song she told me about, "John Jacob Jingleheimerschmidt" that he also reacted to, but not in a good way. If I started singing it, he would shake his head and start to cry. V thought maybe it had been a song we sang to him, and that was why he reacted that way. I told her I couldn't remember ever singing that to him, and we were both confused about his reaction. In retrospect, I wonder if Kim sang it to him in the hospital or one of the nurses. Who knows?

Jacob rode the short bus to school and we started having problems almost immediately. There were two stretches of road where he would react to something and would thrash about in his wheelchair, pull his hair, hit his head, pinch his face and scream. We tried sending him with toys or magazines, even his favorite swimsuit issue, but he wouldn't be distracted. Every time he went past the Pulp Mill and the power station, he went crazy. Since Jacob was still recovering from major craniofacial reconstruction surgery and had lots of little plates and screws holding the delicate grafts together, we had to do something for his own protection. Dean came up with an idea that was ludicrous but nevertheless seemed to work for the most part. We got a motorcycle helmet and decorated the visor with all sorts of visual and tactile objects to distract him. Even if he wasn't always distracted, at least his head was protected.

At first, it was only on the bus that he reacted, but it wasn't long before we saw the same behavior in the car. It was scary how intensely he reacted. He seemed to be experiencing physical pain. We figured it had to have something to do with high pitch noises, but it wasn't like we could just avoid these places as it was the only way into town. We finally got a referral to a behavior therapist in the lower 48 to see if he could help. I was really skeptical of some guy thousands of miles away and having no idea of who Jacob was being able to figure all this out. He started out by having us fill out a card each time Jacob reacted. It showed where we were, who was there, what Jacob did, and how we tried to calm him. We started filling out cards until we had a few weeks' worth. After he reviewed them, he gave us some things to try. We were eventually able to get Jacob to keep his hands down when he started losing it. It kept him focused on his hands which lessened the thrashing and it kept him from pulling his hair and hitting himself. We never did get to a point where he could ignore it completely, but the tantrums got less and less with calm assurances and the "hands down" reminder. The aide on the short bus also saw improvement when she used the same reminders.

Sometimes when Jacob was on the verge of losing, it, we would try anything to distract him. I remember two occasions when the results were somewhat humorous. Once Michelle gave him a can of Coke, his favorite, with about an inch in the bottom. He wanted so badly to throw the can, but it was Coke, so he would take a drink, then scream, take another drink, and scream again. I don't know how he didn't manage to choke on it. Another time Michelle gave him a

Tylenol bottle which he would normally love to shake, but he was so agitated he started hitting himself with it. Then when he heard the rattle, he would stop and then start up again. It was so funny I couldn't stop laughing long enough to take it from him.

The travel issue was a huge one for our family, as everyone was affected. Everyone in the vehicle started tensing up as we neared the trigger spots. One night I was coming home late from town, and Jacob started in. Since I was driving, there was no way I could keep him calm, so I just gritted my teeth and sped up to get through it. Unfortunately, there was a cop and I got pulled over. I remember pulling out my paperwork and waiting for my ticket while Jacob howled and thrashed for all he was worth. Michelle sat in her seat with her eyes wide open, not saying a word. The cop came up to the window, took my papers, looked at Michelle and Jacob, gave me my papers, told me to slow down and went back to his car. I guess he could tell a woman on edge and figured a ticket might just push me right over that edge.

Jacob was very tactile. One of his favorite things was the cellophane windows in envelopes. He loved the crinkly sound it made. He also loved anything laminated. Dean would let him play with his license until he started separating the laminated layers. One time Dean was letting him play with his hand until he realized Jacob was separating his fingernail layers. That poor fingernail is deformed to this day.

Not long after school started, his class was performing a talent show, and the parents were invited to attend. I couldn't imagine what Jacob would be doing, and Auntie G wouldn't tell me. So we showed up with no idea what to expect. With G and Jacob involved, it could be anything. When all the kids came on stage to do a song and dance number, there was our Jacob standing proudly with his little man walker. When the dance started, he did a slow turn with his partner. He was slow and meticulous, and I could hear his happy noise as he did his thing. It was perfect, and I was one proud Mama.

Jacob was accepted at school and had lots of little friends. G told me it was hard to get him down the hallway because everyone wanted to stop and say "Hi."

His popularity began to follow us around town as well. We were often stopped by kids wanting to say "Hi" and introduce Jacob to their parents or siblings. It was a welcome change.

When it came time for school pictures, we were excited. We dressed Jacob up and gave him a haircut. When the pictures finally came back, I went to get them and found G and C acting a little weird. When I looked at the pictures, I knew why. The photographer was apparently wigged out by Jacob and took a picture of him looking up with his arm in front of his face. I couldn't believe it. I was so ticked off.

Even though Keagan was thrilled to have Jacob around, he still struggled with Dean and me. When he was about three, he got mad because we wouldn't let him have candy, and he threw a fit. We sent him to his room to calm down and sat at the table discussing his behavior. After a bit, Dean looked out the window and saw a small figure walking up the hill from the dock. There is a little store there where the kids liked to get candy and snacks. Dean said it looked like Keagan, but I couldn't believe it. We watched him and sure enough, it was him. He had left through the downstairs door and walked to the store by himself. We waited for him and foolishly expected him to show a repentant attitude. Instead, he marched up to us boldly and said since we wouldn't let him have any candy, he got his own, and we couldn't take it from him because he bought it with his own money.

Dean and I decided to get a boat since we lived on an island. We bought a 23' cabin cruiser and a dinghy. We went fishing, camped out, explored, went swimming and threw Dean overboard to get us crab. That boat was such a stress reducer. Jacob loved the motion, especially when the weather was rough. Dean taught Keagan to fish with a bail reel and was surprised at how quickly he picked it up.

Keagan loved it. We also set shrimp pots, and the kids were always excited to see what we caught when we pulled them up. We would take the boat to Yes Bay to set our gill net for sockeye salmon. Keagan loved to help pull the fish up and he was good at it. We finally found something that really interested him. At first, Michelle loved the boat and was as excited as we were to be out on it. Later it was, "Why do I have to go? I want to go see my friends." We usually brought her friends along if we could, but that boat made life so much more bearable. To be able to get away, no phones, no appointments, just peace.

Keagan's anger became such an ordeal. We never knew when he would react or how to get him to calm down. He broke one of his sister's toy horses because she made him mad. She'd been collecting these since she was little, so she was pretty upset. We hoped to teach him a lesson by letting her take one of his toys. It didn't make the right impact because all he did was get angrier. He got revenge by stabbing her in the leg with a pen knife. Again, he felt completely justified. He believed he was the only one who had any right to control his life. He didn't want or need parents, and he resented the fact that we could make decisions for him. It was so confusing to us, and we really didn't know what to do.

Michelle had hit the boy stage and it brought even more complications to an already complicated life. We lived a block away from her school, so we frequently had her friends over after school. Keagan loved being around the teens and thought he was one of them. These were the kids he wanted to invite to his birthday party. Dean wasn't such a fan of the boys and they usually scattered when he got home.

We got a call from G; Jacob had fallen at school and was hurt. I went to the school and got the story. Jacob had been outside on the playground with his walker. He tripped and fell. Because he always covered the top of his head when he felt threatened, he didn't put his hands in front of himself and hit his face full-on. He ended up losing a couple of teeth and had some scrapes and bruises, but that was it. I really didn't think it was that big of a deal, just a playground accident, but G was really shaken up. She just knew she would be blamed for letting him fall. I couldn't imagine anybody trying to hold her responsible. I was wrong. As soon as the dentist bills hit Medicaid, I got all kinds of inquiries about who was to blame, whose fault it was, who should have protected him, and how this could have been avoided. It was nonsense. I filled out every inquiry the same way. It was Jacob's fault. He should have protected himself, he should have learned to walk better. Even Kim wanted to know whose fault it was. It was an accident and by nature, accidents aren't anyone's fault.

At four, Keagan tried to set the house on fire because of some perceived injustice. He took a box of matches and tried to set the wood pilings of the house on fire. Fortunately for us, we lived in rainforest and it didn't take. We didn't know about it until I found a pile of burned matches on the ground. When I asked him what was going on, he admitted he'd done it and wasn't one bit sorry. I tried to explain the consequences of what would have happened if he'd been successful, but he wasn't fazed. He was mad, and he wanted to hurt us all.

Keagan had a friend over to play one day. He and Dan were in the bedroom playing, so I assumed everything was fine. Dan was a nice kid, and they were laughing so I didn't pay them much attention. Then Keagan brought out my pet rabbit and told me it was hurt. He initially said he didn't know what had happened but finally admitted that he and Dan had been playing with it when it went all floppy. Later I found out they had been throwing it against the wall until they broke its neck. When I confronted him, he said it wasn't his fault. The rabbit just got hurt. No remorse, no apology, just indifference and an attitude that said I dare you to get angry at me.

In between the scary "my son is a sociopath moments" there were other times his behavior was sometimes funny and even a little sad.

For all his smarts, he had difficulty understanding relationships. He couldn't get how my Dad was his grandfather. Also, why couldn't he marry me when he got older? Daddy had.

There was also Keagan in the Mirror. In my bedroom, the closet doors were mirrored, and they were huge, so basically, one wall was mirrored. Keagan had been in my room many times, but this day he saw his reflection and stopped in his tracks. He looked at me and asked, "Who is that?" I thought he was playing a game, so I said, "That's Keagan in the Mirror. Why don't you say Hi?" He slowly turned back, said Hi, and waved. He was so surprised I realized he was serious. "Look, he waved back at me!"

After that day, whenever he came into my room, he would have a little meet and greet with Keagan in the Mirror.

He was also terrified of "the criminals." If he heard a strange noise, he would immediately hide under the bed or in a closet because he knew it was the criminals. We have no idea where that one came from, but it lasted until his pre-teen years.

Keagan was really smart. He frequently picked up on things that a small child shouldn't. We learned that nothing was safe with Keagan around.

Dean and I were playing cards at the kitchen table one day, and Keagan went down to the shop. He was often out there with Papa since Papa now lived in his house over the shop. Shortly he came into the workroom where Dean had his tools and then went back out again. After this happened a few times, Dean went to see what he was doing. When he got out to the shop, he found Keagan on Papa's old tractor with a screwdriver in the ignition, trying to start it. He knew that was how Papa started it but didn't know what size screwdriver to use. He was pretty close to figuring it out when Dean found him. That's when the tools started getting locked up.

When we were having some work done on the driveway, Miles left the equipment parked in the driveway overnight. Keagan had been watching him the previous day and saw where he hid the key. When Dean found him, he had the key in the ignition and was trying to start it to go for a ride. Thank goodness he didn't see Miles disconnect the battery before he left.

Keagan's best friend was the neighbor girl Missy. She would often come over to play, and it was really cute to overhear them playing princess and hero. One day we heard Keagan respond, I'm not being the hero today; I was the hero yesterday. Today I'm being a dinosaur. Apparently, they traded days, heroes one day, dinosaurs the next. Missy's parents liked Keagan. One day he went over to play with Missy, and she wasn't home, so he spent the entire day hanging out with her dad in his garage. Another time Missy's mom woke up and found Keagan sitting in her living room. She asked him what he was doing, and he said he was waiting for Missy to get up. She turned on the TV and made him breakfast. He never told us about any of this, just said he was playing with Missy. I can't imagine what they thought about us as parents.

1995

Keagan went to preschool. He started attending the same school as his sister. We hoped it would be a good experience for him and teach him a little self-discipline and how to interact appropriately with others. It ended up being a difficult year with lots of phone calls and being called to the school to intervene. He just wouldn't behave. One day after school, he showed up with a little girl. I asked him what was going on and he said he asked her to come play. I freaked out and called the school because I had no idea who this child was and was pretty sure her parents didn't know where she was. Sure enough, her dad was at the school, and they were about to call the police. The whole school staff was out looking for her. When her dad arrived, I apologized profusely, but I could see in his eyes that his daughter would be told to stay far away from "that kid." Keagan became the kid that other parents warned their kids about.

Keagan was often angry and primarily at me. He started hurling verbal spears that he knew would hurt me. My only defense was not to take the bait. He told me he couldn't ever trust me because I had lied to him and that he had to take care of himself because he couldn't trust me to take care of him. This was followed by, "I want to live with the mother who birthed me." I wanted to tell him that the mother that birthed him was the one he hid from at the fruit stand, but I didn't. Instead of responding emotionally, I simply told him he couldn't. The courts wouldn't allow him to, and he was stuck being a McFarland until he was 18. I'm pretty sure he started counting the days from that moment.

One day at church, the secretary came up to me to tell me about a new family moving to Ketchikan. She was so excited because she just knew we were going to be great friends because they had a special needs child too. I immediately got offended. I am so much more than the mom with that kid, and I can pick out my own friends, thank you very much. I made up my mind that I wasn't going to have anything to do with them when they came.

When the McGuffey's did arrive and I saw their boy David my heart was touched. David was so beautiful. He was also a dwarf with lots of health problems that came with that. I got to know the family and fell in love with each and every one of them.

Our families became very close, and when they needed a place to stay for a time, we opened our home. I discussed it with my Pastor before-hand, and he advised me to be careful. He said, "This will either end your friendship or bond your families for life." I'm thankful it ended up being the latter.

When the McGuffey's moved in, there were five of them and five of us. Lawana and I took care of the kids while Dean and Clint headed off to work. Keagan and Isaiah butted heads more than they got along, but the babies were awesome. By now, David was two, Mary Hannah was one, and Jacob was six. I know six isn't a baby, but Jacob kind of was always my baby. We had so much fun that summer. One day we filled up hundreds of water balloons, and when the guys came home from work, we met them with a barrage from the upper deck. We were nice, though, we did put a couple of buckets on the driveway for them. I still remember Clint trying to catch them in his baseball glove. When they moved to Prince of Wales, they left a huge hole.

As time went on, Jacob's parents became more difficult to work with. So many appointments were canceled. They couldn't or wouldn't agree on what needed to happen with him. There were threats and accusations, and nothing was happening for our boy. Finally, the State of Alaska had enough and they filed a petition with the courts for a medical <u>Guardian Ad Litem</u> to be appointed to make medical decisions for Jacob.

I knew once the paperwork was filed that if we didn't win Kim would take Jacob away from us as punishment. Even though we hadn't filed the suit, we were definitely on the GAL side.

I took Jacob to court with me. I figured the whole thing was about him, and the people at the hearing needed to be reminded of that. George was there with his lawyer, but Kim was there by phone. She was now living in Washington. Her mother was also in court. The first day the judge told me Jacob couldn't be there. I had to leave and have a friend come get him for the day. Apparently, the judge was so upset over his appearance that he wouldn't allow him to be there. The testimony given wasn't really about Jacob and what was best for him. Instead, it was days of back-and-forth accusations, and he said, she said. The parents maintained their victim status by saying everyone had taken advantage of them and kept them from their son. I was accused of lying, being only in it for the money, making it difficult for them to see their son, and not caring about Jacob. My journal came into play, and it helped a bit, but the whole thing was just so ugly. Finally, on the third day, George said that all he and Kim ever wanted was to take their boy home and that they were never allowed to do so. The judge reminded him that he had retained custody throughout Jacob's life and could have taken him home at any time. George responded that he'd been threatened by the hospital and Community Connections that if he tried to take Jacob home, he would lose him. It didn't make any sense, but the judge assured him he could take Jacob if that was what he wanted. Kim agreed this had always been their desire. The judge dismissed the case, and George made plans to take Jacob.

After his ruling, the judge said that if the state had filed a <u>CINA petition,</u> he would have granted it, but since they hadn't, he had no choice. He also told George that he had better take good care of Jacob because he would be watched by <u>CPS</u>. I found out that is a bunch of rubbish. Each state operates independently, and once you leave one state, there are no records forwarded. Unless you have a complaint filed in your new state, there is no one monitoring the child's well-being.

Jacob was on IV antibiotics for a staph infection at his Mic-Key site at the time of the hearing. After the judge dismissed the case, I picked him up and took him to Dr. J for his final treatment. I broke down as I told him about the outcome. I was devastated. I couldn't believe what had happened. What was going to become of him? How could this be justice? Poor Dr. J just sat there and listened while I vented and sobbed.

George agreed to spend a couple of days familiarizing himself with Jacob's care before he took him. That didn't happen. He called the next day and said his lawyer told him he didn't have to spend time with us if he didn't want to. He would come to get Jacob the following day. When he came, he only wanted the necessities. We tried to talk to him about sending Jacob's things to Kim, but he wasn't interested. He left everything else, took Jacob, and was gone. We heard he literally got on a plane, dropped Jacob off with Kim, and then returned home, so much for wanting his son.

Jacob was gone. We donated all his toys, appliances, supplies, machines, wheelchair, furniture and clothes. Everything but his baby book. I needed to make sure I wasn't accused of profiting off of Jacob since that accusation had been tossed around in court. I was heartbroken for Jacob. I can't imagine what he thought was going on. These people were strangers to him, knew nothing about him, and had resented his life since the day he was born. And now they were his primary caregivers.

1996

We heard there were concerns raised by Jacob's new school, and a complaint was made. CPS in Washington had opened a file and was looking into things when Kim moved to California. Apparently, she knew CPS records don't follow you when you relocate to another state.

Keagan's Kindergarten year was a challenge for both of us. The preschool he'd attended was a small, private school, and that hadn't turned out great, but this was the real deal. Keagan had issues with authority figures, and this carried over to this school. We got called frequently. It wasn't only that he wouldn't do what was asked; it was the defiance that came with it. He threatened people who weren't being nice to him, swore when talking to the teacher (thanks, Papa), and brought a weapon to school (a 3/4" pen knife). In other words, typical Keagan.

Dean and I took a trip to see Jacob. We hadn't seen him in almost a year, and we were anxious to know if he was okay, really okay. Kim was agreeable and allowed us to take Jacob for the day. Jacob knew us immediately, and he was so happy. It was such a beautiful time. We spent the day having fun with our boy. We took him shopping, to the playground, got ice cream and spent hours back at the hotel just loving on him and playing with him. When we left, we thought maybe he would be all right. We went home hopeful.

I got a call from Angus with <u>DMHDD</u>. He asked me if I would be willing to talk to a young mother in Anchorage who had a newborn with developmental issues. Apparently, she had little support and was finding it difficult to deal with everything. He couldn't share anything that might be considered confidential, so that was pretty much what I got. I told him that was fine and he said he would give my number to the mom, and she would call me if she wanted to. It wasn't long before she called. Her little girl was terminal, and she was struggling with the thought of finding her dead. That was understandable, but since it was unavoidable, I didn't really know what I could say that would make any difference. I tried to encourage her to enjoy the time she had with her, but it was really tearing her apart. So I ended up being a sounding board for her, and eventually, she decided she just couldn't do it. After about a week, she asked me if I would take her baby. I agreed, and plans were made to go to Anchorage. I honestly didn't know how I would handle finding a newborn dead in her crib, but I couldn't not help her. I hoped that the small degree of separation of not being her birth mother would make it marginally easier for me.

I called Angus, and he started making plans to bring the baby girl to Ketchikan. Before I left, I contacted Dr. J and filled him in on our newest family member. He arranged to get her records so he would be ready when we got her home.

Dean and I flew to Anchorage. We were met by Lee with <u>DFYS</u>. She was Jenny's caseworker. We went to a round table with doctors, therapists, and others involved with Jenny's care. They explained her condition (<u>Alobar Holoprosencephaly</u> and seizures) and how it affected her daily care. She had no upper palate, so she couldn't be fed with a bottle. She was currently being fed with an eye dropper. Where her upper palate should have been, she had nasal passages, so we had to make sure the food didn't get into her airway. They considered doing a g-tube, but since her life expectancy was very short, they opted not to. It was the comfort vs. function discussion again. She was basically <u>anencephalic,</u> and the opinion was that her central nervous system would just shut down, and it would be sooner rather than later. She also had constant seizures and was on medication for them. After they explained all this, they still seemed reluctant for us to take Jenny and kept emphasizing her issues and prognosis. Finally, Dean asked if I had a picture of Jacob. I did, and as I started to pass it around, Dean explained that this had been our previous foster child. I filled them in on his primary diagnosis, and by the time it made its way back to me, everyone was on board.

Tammy, Jenny's mother, was really sweet. I was surprised by how young she was. She was a beautiful Inupiaq woman who also had two rambunctious boys. Her boyfriend was quite a bit older and denied he was Jenny's father. When I saw they were native, the whole thing made a little more sense. Their culture looks at things a little differently than I do. I asked Tammy again if this was what she wanted, and she assured me that it was. It was hard because I genuinely believed she was making a decision she would regret later on. Regardless of how difficult things are, once they're gone, all you have are memories, and she was handing hers off to me.

We caught the plane home with our sweet little baby girl. Auntie G and C had planned a welcome baby shower for Jenny. They wanted to do it to help welcome her and also because you never know what's coming with kids when you take them in. By the time we got home, Jenny's body temperature had dropped dangerously low, and I thought she was dying. I called Dr. J, and he recommended body-to-body contact. At least, it would make her feel more comfortable. He agreed with me that she was probably shutting down. We canceled the shower, and I stripped her down and cuddled with her. By bedtime, her temperature came back up, and she seemed fine. The next few days were busy trying to make adjustments for all the changes a new baby brings. Because of Jenny's age and her prognosis, we didn't have the invasion of service providers we had with Jacob. Our days were relatively quiet. Michelle was being home-schooled this year, so she spent a lot of time sitting next to Jenny while she did her school work. Jenny did very little, and Michelle loved having her cuddle up next to her.

One of Michelle's classes was Creative Writing. Since her papers were graded remotely, I didn't always see them before they were sent off. When she got a packet of scored papers returned, I found one with a small rosebud painted on it with an essay she'd written about Jenny. It was really sweet and talked about a beautiful rosebud that had so much potential yet didn't get to bloom. It remained forever a rosebud.

It was beautiful and reminded me again of how insightful Michelle was.

Keagan showed little, if any, interest in Jenny. We still went out in the boat as often as we could, and Jenny was right there with us in a snugglie. I remember Dean pushing Keagan on a rope swing we found on an island with Jenny strapped to his chest. Or another time, we were sneaking up on sea lions, and their roar startled her. Where we went, she went. That's just how we lived.

Jenny was around six weeks old when she came to live with us. She was easy to care for but did develop one quirk that was overwhelming. It started shortly after we got home and continued almost every single night. She would start screaming around 11 pm and would continue non-stop until around 4:30 in the morning. She was absolutely inconsolable. The only thing that helped was to rock her and pat her back. Most nights, I sat up with her since I didn't have an outside job. However, I did have Keagan and Michelle, as well as Jenny, to care for. I also had to monitor Michelle's progress on her schoolwork. Every now and then, when I just couldn't do it, Dean would take her so I could get some sleep. He got so good at it that I would find him asleep in the morning with Jenny on his chest, still patting her.

Caring for Jenny was so much easier than caring for Jacob. There was just that little bit of fear about when she died.

Everyone we knew fell in love with our baby girl. She had chubby little cheeks and black hair that stuck out in all directions. Only those close to us understood how very fragile she was.

As the weeks went by, we sort of pushed the whole dying thing to the back of our minds until one night when it all came crashing back. Auntie G was babysitting for us, but when we got home, the house was in a panic. Jenny had quit breathing, and G called an ambulance. Dean and I headed into the hospital and found her in the ER. She was breathing and seemed fine. When the doctor came in, I spent 20 minutes explaining to him what was going on. Finally, we took her home no worse for wear.

Dean headed to Prince of Wales Island for his annual hunting trip. Two days later, Jenny stopped breathing again. Michelle was doing her schoolwork with Jenny beside her, and she called me when she realized she wasn't breathing. She went to call 911, and I started doing rescue breathing. Jenny started breathing again. When the ambulance came, we told them she was fine, but they said once they were called, they were required to transport the patient. So off we went to the hospital. Once again, I explained the situation, and the doctor listened patiently. Then we had the discussion I'd been avoiding. She asked me why I resuscitated her when I knew her condition was terminal. The only answer I could give her was that I wasn't really thinking, just reacting. So we had a long discussion about her prognosis and the futility of trying to keep her alive through resuscitation. We agreed that I would not revive her again, and she updated Dr. J.

I got in touch with Tammy and updated her on everything that had happened. I told her that it wouldn't be long and she should be prepared. I also contacted my dear friend Clint on Prince of Wales. He knew where Dean hunted and agreed to try and find him and let him know what was happening.

The next day Jenny quit eating. She gagged when I tried to feed her. She wouldn't swallow, and the formula would just pool up in her mouth. She also quit seizing and night time crying. Dr. J said to just keep her comfortable. So I put her in the snugglie and kept her with me. I used a small bottle of water to spritz her mouth, and that was pretty much all I could do for her. I continued to take care of the kids but always with Jenny in my arms or in the snugglie.

The afternoon of the second day, it was just Jenny and I rocking, and I felt the presence of my Great Grandmother. This beautiful woman had been a source of comfort and an example of unconditional love for me. She died when I was 12, and although I often thought of her, I had never felt her presence as I did that day. It was as if she was standing right next to me. I began to talk to her and told her about Jenny. I told her Jenny was coming soon and asked her to look after her. It was such a beautiful experience, and it left me more accepting of what was coming.

I spent the next day and a half talking to Jenny. I told her how precious she was and reminded her that she was loved. I talked to her about anything and everything. I wanted her to know I was right there with her.

Clint found Dean, and he was coming home that evening. I took Jenny to the school basketball game just to get out of the house. While I was there, I told her about what was happening and reminded her that everything was going to be okay. As I was getting ready to head home, a man walked up to me. He was a believer and said that God wanted me to know that He was pleased with me.

When I got home, I handed Jenny to Michelle and went to put my things away. Shortly after I came back into the room, Dean arrived. He walked into the living room, still carrying all his hunting gear, and went straight to Michelle. He kissed Jenny on the forehead and said, "There's my girl." He turned to put his things away, and Michelle quietly walked over to me and whispered, "She quit breathing." I took her and held her as she passed from life to death.

I tried to call Tammy, but her line was busy. After several attempts, I finally called the operator and asked her to interrupt the call. She asked me if it was an emergency, and it took me by surprise. I thought about it and realized it wasn't really since nothing would change in 10 minutes, but yes, it was because she needed to know. I finally got through to her, and she was already crying. She told me she didn't want to answer the phone because she knew what she was going to hear. We talked until she was good, and she told me what arrangements she wanted me to make for Jenny.

Then I called Dana, the hospice lady, who had agreed to come to get Jenny when she died. She came out to the house, and when we were all done loving on her and ready to let her go, she took her little body to the funeral home.

When I look back on that night, I don't remember anyone being there but Michelle, Dean, myself and Jenny. Michelle insists that the aunties and our pastor, and his wife were there. But somehow, I don't remember them at all and can't imagine who would have notified them. I don't even know where Keagan was. Grief is weird.

The next day we met with the funeral director and took an outfit for her to be buried in. The arrangement was to have her body shipped to Anchorage, where her mom was making funeral arrangements. We had a small memorial service for her at our church. Michelle pretty much took the lead with the planning, and she did a great job. I spent my time walking around with Jenny's satin pillow that I was convinced smelled like her.

After the service, we all headed to Prince of Wales. Dean rejoined his hunting party, and the kids and I spent a few days with Clint. It was good to get away and grieve in private.

Several weeks later, we flew to Anchorage and stopped by to see Jenny's grave. Tammy has a picture of Jenny on the tombstone, our sweet little baby girl. We were even able to spend some time with Tammy and the boys, and it was good to know they were all doing okay.

1997

In June, the Pulp Mill shut down, and Dean got a job in Fairbanks with Alaska Airlines. We sold our boat and packed up the house, and headed north. We stayed with Grandma Margie, Dean's mother, initially but eventually bought a small house in North Pole. Keagan and Michelle were both angry about the move. Michelle, at 15, was losing all her friends and she resented us for causing this. I could have explained that it wasn't our fault that the mill shut down and her dad had to find work where he could get it, but it wouldn't have mattered.

I was 15 when my mom dragged me kicking and screaming from Texas to Alaska, so I completely understood.

Keagan was mad because we were leaving everything he loved behind; fishing, crabbing, beach combing and Papa. Keagan was a difficult child and Papa was one of the few adults that he actually cared about.

Fortunately, he connected with Grandma Margie and JB, her husband. He also had his Uncle Craig living right around the corner. Dean and I were interested to see how their relationship would develop since Craig is every bit as strong-willed as Keagan. It was entertaining watching an eight-year-old and a 37-year-old battle it out. Craig is a grown-up Keagan and totally intolerant of Keagan-like behavior. One day Keagan walked over to visit Uncle Craig, who lived a block away and came back after only a few minutes. We asked him what had happened, and he told us Craig had told him to leave. When we asked Craig about it, he said Keagan was being mouthy and rude, and he did indeed tell him to leave his house. They spent some time together, and Craig enjoyed his intelligence and out-of-the-box thinking, but when he started acting out, he was done.

While we were waiting for our house to close, I ended up driving the kids to school in North Pole. Keagan started 1st grade and I was hopeful it wouldn't be a repeat of the last two years. Because of the issues we'd had previously and the fact that I didn't want to drive the 15 miles back and forth to Fairbanks, I became a school volunteer. I spent my days xeroxing, laminating and cutting things out. I was also on hand when there were issues with Keagan. His teacher was a really nice lady. She was a pastor's wife, and she truly liked Keagan. She wouldn't, however, put up with any nonsense. She told me there were many mornings when he would walk in, and she would take one look at him and could see the storm brewing. She would take him aside and ask him if he really wanted to go there. Sometimes he was able to shake it off and the day was pretty good. Other days... Well, that's the reason I became their favorite volunteer.

Jacob is dead. I got a phone call from JoAnna at Community Connections to let me know Jacob has died. There are no details, so I assumed he died by aspiration, as this is so common with children with compromised respiratory systems. Of course, it could have been his central nervous system just shutting down. With Jacob's unusual anatomy, the doctors predicted he wouldn't live past 12. Of course, these were the same doctors who predicted he wouldn't live to 1. But today, it's real, he is dead. We sent a card to Kim to let her know our prayers were with her.

During this time, we re-connected with Pastor W. He was now at the North Pole Assembly of God. I told him about Jacob and he was pretty upset. That boy affected so many people. We began to attend his church and before long, I was teaching Children's Church.

When we finally got into our house, life became so much easier. All of our goods had been in storage for so long that it was like rediscovering treasure as we unpacked. As I got around to unpacking our pictures, I came across a framed 8x10 of Jacob, and as I looked at it, I could smell him. That very specific smell of his. A combination of pediasure, glycerin swabs and an open mouth breather. At that moment, I knew without a doubt that he hadn't died peacefully as his body simply shut down. He died violently, and everything in me knew Kim was responsible. I could feel his terror as his life was taken from him and he fought to live. I shared it with Dean, but we had no way to get more information, so we waited. About a week later, the call came. JoAnna from Community Connections called and asked if I was alone. She wanted to call back when Dean was home, but I insisted she tell me what she knew. Jacob had been suffocated by his mother. The ME found blanket fibers in his throat. Kim was questioned by the police. Her version was that Jacob, somehow, rolled onto his stomach and was unable to lift his face off the blanket and suffocated. She neglected to call the authorities for 18 hours because she wanted time to say goodbye.

Jacob, by this time, could roll over, do somersaults, crawl and walk. There is no way he suffocated by accident. The 18 hours is very interesting since she had her three other children in the house to care for. Seriously if you found your child unconscious, wouldn't you call 911 immediately?

I talked to the ME. He said he knew Jacob was suffocated, but because of his unusual anatomy, he could not say 100% that he was murdered; therefore, the autopsy was inconclusive.

I spoke to the police. They believed without a doubt that Kim killed Jacob. They were questioning her and felt they were close to a confession when Claire brought a lawyer in and stopped the questioning.

I spoke to the DA, and because the autopsy was inconclusive, they opted not to bring any charges against her.

Kim changed her phone number to an unlisted one and moved to another state. Claire changed her number to an unlisted one as well.

Jacob was cremated and his ashes were scattered in SE Alaska, where his father still lived.

I contacted V to make sure she knew what had happened. She told me they had been contacted by Kim a couple of months before he died. Apparently, she was finding it difficult to cope with caring for Jacob. She asked them to take him for a time. After struggling with the decision, they told her they would only take him if she relinquished her parental rights. She refused and that was the last they heard from her.

I spent the next year in unimaginable grief and anger. I tried to find Kim. I wanted her to know that I knew what she had done. I was determined that in as much as it was possible, I would hold her accountable even if no one else would. As I spun my wheels that year, the anger became like cancer. It almost consumed me. Even as I write this, I am shaking at the unfairness of it all. Jacob had two families that loved him, and she would not allow either one of them to have him. She wanted him gone from the moment he took a breath, and now she got her wish.

I started the licensing process when we moved to North Pole. When they came for the inspection, I was not in a good place and they considered not licensing us. We opted instead to just do respite for a while. Respite is much less intense since it isn't full-time. We started watching, among others, three boys who became like part of the family. They would come out once a month and spend the weekend with us. When they first came, we were warned that they might try and run away. Dean took their shoes and hid them, then told them to have at it. We never had any problems with them. Ben, Adam and Sam were around 12, 10 and 8, and Keagan loved having boys around to play with.

Life carried on. Michelle was in high school. We agreed that she could go to public school for the first time. It was a concession due to the move. We pretty much regretted it right away. Her grades fell, and we had to deal with uncooperative teachers and, of course, school drama. Keagan was in 1st grade, and I spent the days I wasn't doing Respite hanging out at his school. Dean liked his new job, but it came at the price of a 50% pay cut, so we had to become creative when it came to having fun.

Life in North Pole is so different from Ketchikan. We definitely were no longer in the rain forest. Here it was so dry the snow wouldn't even stick together. Also, the snow does this weird thing called sublimation, where it goes from a solid to a gas without becoming a liquid. The temperature has ridiculous extremes, from 85 in summer to -75 in winter. Over 100 degrees variation. We also get the midnight sun here. In summer, you'll see families out at 2 am going on a bike ride. Of course, that comes with the winter darkness that wreaks havoc on those struggling with depression.

We were anxious to discover what our new home had to offer. The kids got bikes and eventually four-wheelers and a snow machine. We spent summer time looking for places to try our hand at gold panning. We went berry picking for blueberries and, after the first frost, cranberries. We got the kids a trampoline for the summer and sleds for the winter. Keagan was introduced to hockey, and even though he didn't know how to skate, he picked it up pretty quickly.

We were also involved in the church. Some of the first people we met at church were the Grants. When we were introduced, Bea made a beeline for us. She asked us if we were "The McFarlands." I wasn't sure what she meant. She explained that Pastor W had often spoken of the McFarlands who took care of Jacob. Apparently, they'd heard all about us before we even knew we were moving. I told her we were, and she was fascinated. She and I became friends and before we knew it, we were having her family, all 7 of them, over to play cards in our tiny 800 sq. ft. house. We were so packed in we had to climb over each other to get to the bathroom.

1998

The following November, I chaperoned a bunch of teens to Anchorage for a youth convention. The kids were wild, the music was loud, and the atmosphere was electric. I loved it. One evening during the worship service, God spoke to me. "You're done" was all I heard, but I instantly felt the burden lift. I felt reassured that God would bring justice where the courts failed. That God knew Kim's location even though I'd failed to find her. That God would remind her of Jacob's death, but not with the purpose of vengeance but to lead her to salvation and forgiveness. I was finally free to pray for her and let God be God. It was amazing to feel the bands on my heart loosen so I could breathe again. I could look at Jacob's picture and remember how happy and precious he was. I could live again.

Jacob was never a pretty child, but his giggles, his laughter, and his joy made him beautiful. I feel sorry for people who can't see past outward appearances. They miss so much.

When Michelle started 10th grade, I steeled myself for another year of academic probation, counselors who were convinced they knew my child better than me and uncooperative teachers. On the 10th day of school, I had to go in to pay a class fee. I also thought I'd check on Michelle as she hadn't been feeling great that morning. As I pulled into the parking lot, I was surprised to see her run out the doors and straight to her boyfriend's car. I watched her hop in and they took off. Michelle wasn't allowed to leave campus, and Dan, who was out of school, was certainly not allowed to take her anywhere without our permission. So I had some thinking to do. After a little while, I went into the school and took care of business. Then I returned to my car and waited. When I saw them pull in, I waited until Dan left and then called out to Michelle. She immediately knew she was busted. I asked her if she'd had a nice lunch, and she said she had. I then told her to go in and get her things. When she asked why I told her she'd been un-enrolled.

We got Michelle enrolled in home school and things seemed to settle down for a bit. However, it wasn't long before she was in trouble again with Dan. We tried to limit their contact to church and group activities but they started sneaking around and lying about it. Her biggest mistake was letting Dan bribe Keagan to keep quiet. He couldn't wait to tell. I think he enjoyed not being the one in trouble too much to keep quiet. Anyway, we decided Michelle needed a reality check.

We made arrangements with Lawana and shipped Michelle off to stay with her family for a couple of months. It really wasn't a punishment, especially going to Lawana's, but just a chance for her to get some perspective with a wise woman who loved her. We also knew that Dan would have no way of contacting her on a float-house, in Naukiti Bay, on Prince of Wales Island.

When it was time to go get her, Keagan and I went together. We had a great time reconnecting with our McFamily. When we visited their church on Sunday, something wonderful happened.

I sent Keagan to the children's church and hoped for the best. He was usually on good behavior when Lawana was around. She kept him in line by telling him she had a lightbulb that went off in her head when she was lied to. He wasn't sure if she did, but he wasn't willing to take a chance.

When class was over, I saw him coming towards me with his teacher. I steeled myself for the worst. She came to ask me if she could give him a book. She'd read the book to the class and Keagan was really affected by it. She wanted to give it to him as a gift. The book was one I hadn't read, "You Are Special" by Max Lucado. The book is about a puppet that seeks approval from others until he finally meets his creator and realizes he already has his approval. It's a good book and Keagan still has the book to this day.

We finally got our first full-time foster child since moving to North Pole. We signed up for regular foster care, but once they knew our background, we were pegged as special needs foster parents. Emma was ten, but she was so thin and emaciated that she looked more like five. She had <u>Cerebral Palsy</u> and <u>microcephaly</u>. The school had reported her to CPS because she was starving and had started to eat her own hair. She also came to school dirty and unkempt. When we took her, we were told she could only eat oatmeal and rice. Not because of allergies but because that was all she would eat. The first evening we took her shopping to get some clothes that fit her. She'd been wearing a nasty sweat suit many sizes too big. I don't know what it is about sweat suits and special needs kids, but it just makes me angry. It's like they aren't worth taking the time to put real clothes on them.

After shopping, we went out to eat at an all-you-can-eat buffet. Emma was making lots of noise and hand motions when she smelled the food. I gave her a couple of bites of mashed potatoes to see if she would eat them. She swallowed it and whined for more. I continued to feed her off my plate, vegetables, fruit and potatoes. She never was sated but I figured she'd had enough and didn't want her to vomit.

Emma's skin was grey and she smelled awful. Even after a bath, there was a lingering sick smell. It took several weeks for it to go away. We tried everything to get her to quit eating her hair. We hoped she'd stop when she was getting adequate nutrition, but she didn't. I finally got permission from her mother to cut it. She looked super cute but got a little confused and frustrated when she would try to pull it into her mouth. Because of her CP, Emma would literally have to be unknotted each morning before I could get her dressed for school. She still wore diapers, and for some reason, the school decided it was undignified to lay her down for diaper changes. They would instead stand her up and try to pry her stiff legs apart to get the diaper on. After several days of her coming home in someone else's lost clothing, I told them to stop it. It was more undignified to have her pee all over herself and then have to be dressed in whatever they had on hand and smell like urine for the rest of the day.

Keagan was so tied up inside he was constantly looking for ways to release all that pent up anger and frustration. He started urinating in his room and smearing feces on the walls at home and school. We had finally reached our limit.

We contacted a psychologist who agreed to see Keagan. Dr. Matt was a godsend. He listened to us and didn't treat us like we were overreacting or imagining behavior. He also genuinely liked Keagan.

Dr. Matt evaluated Keagan and ran lots of tests. He was diagnosed with <u>Clinical Depression</u> and <u>ADD</u>. We were sent to a doctor for prescriptions, and started family counseling. He also did an IQ test which came back with a score of 138. An IQ over 130 is considered superior. He told us this would probably make things even more difficult. It did. There were many years we heard, "Why won't you listen to me since I'm smarter than you."

I appreciated that Dr. Matt listened and tried to help us problem-solve. He gave me his behavior modification system, "Mother Rules," which the kids still despise to this day. It is a system where house rules are clearly defined and agreed on, with consequences, also clearly defined, for breaking the rules. Also, rewards for following rules. Since it was all agreed on beforehand, it left no room for arguing about fairness and removed the "I didn't know…" excuses. It helped, but the underlying brokenness remained.

1999

Dr. Matt referred us to the Attachment Center in Seattle. We headed down for an evaluation. The doctor spoke to Dean, myself, Michelle and Keagan.

We had all filled out questionnaires before the evaluation, which were then reviewed by the doctors. We were then asked about our home life, and the picture was pretty bleak. One small child was controlling the entire family and we didn't know how to stop it.

The conclusion was that Keagan had attachment issues and should continue counseling.

We started Keagan on medication for ADD. When he took it, he was a different person. He was talkative, he could focus, and he would verbalize frustrations. It was amazing. Unfortunately, it made him not want to eat. It also made him jittery, which he hated. Then there were the frequent blood tests that were terrifying for him. He frequently fainted and would fight me every time we had to go in.

By this time, Keagan's diagnoses had stretched to include ADD, RAD, ODD, Clinical Depression, hyper-vigilance and Hyperacusis.

His frustrations continued to escalate to the point we were considering sending him to a boy's home. It was horrible. Here we had taken this prayed-for little boy into our home and now we were seriously considering sending him away. I felt like such a failure. I tried my own version of holding therapy one afternoon when he was out of control. I held on with everything I had while I asked God to help me help him. He fought me like his life was on the line. I finally let him go and he ran off to his room while I sat there and sobbed. Eventually, it came down to me waiting until he was asleep, then standing by his bedside and praying over him. My heart broke for him because he fought so hard to keep everyone at arm's length. He was so utterly alone and refused to let anyone in. God kept reminding me that He loved Keagan first, He loves him more than I do, and His plans for Keagan were good. I just had to trust Him for his life.

One of the most honest encounters we had started over a tuna sandwich. He didn't want the sandwich and got angry. It escalated to him climbing onto the table and screaming at me. I shouted back, "Why are you doing this?" to which he responded, "I don't know." He was just as confused by his behavior as we were.

The counselors gave us lots of things to try to bring some peace into our home but they only modified behavior; they never reached the heart issue. Michelle was frequently angry with us. She felt like we let him get away with way too much. She wanted us to make him behave. I tried to explain to her that Keagan was like someone who had been in a car crash. Even though he was covered with cuts and bruises, the doctors didn't bother with those because they were concerned with what was going on inside him. Inside he was hemorrhaging to death and they had to stop the bleeding. Once the inside was okay, then they would attend to the cuts and bruises.

His counselor at Hope told me after her initial evaluation that Keagan was the most narcissistic child she'd ever met. I was a little offended by this because I thought of a narcissist as someone who loved themselves and that wasn't Keagan. In fact, I'm pretty sure he hated himself and thought there must be something wrong with him. After thinking about it, I realized she was right. It was my understanding of narcissism that was wrong. It's really about focusing solely on the self. Every time something happened, Keagan ran it through his filter of how it affected him. If it didn't, he didn't care. If it was bad, then someone had to pay. If it was good, then he must have done something to deserve it. He could not believe that someone would do something nice for him without him earning it. He trusted no one but himself. He absolutely believed the world did rotate around him and never considered others' feelings or how his actions affected them.

I remember being asked if I was worried that Keagan would run away. I said, "No. I'm more worried that I'll come home and find he's changed the locks and won't let me in."

There were times Keagan threatened to hurt himself and it scared me, but with Keagan, you can't show fear. When he told me he was going to kill himself, I didn't react. I looked at him and said, "Are you serious? Because if you are, then I'm taking you to the hospital for a psychological evaluation." He then said, "You'd all be happy if I was never born." I assured him that he was loved, he was our answer to prayer and he was very much wanted. He never mentioned suicide again.

Another time he threatened to call CPS to report that he was being abused. He's used this one several times and got the reaction he wanted. As foster parents, a call like that, even if unsubstantiated, would ruin us. I explained that we would lose our license and he would be taken and put with strangers. He didn't care, but since he knew I did, this threat became a regular. However, this time, I took the phone and told him I'd dial for him since I knew the direct number. He glared at me and left the room. No more threats of CPS.

Keagan was a master at pushing people's buttons and the only way to get him to stop was to call his bluff or, as one counselor said, "Just because he casts the hook doesn't mean you have to bite it and swallow. Spit it out and swim on."

As Emma gained weight, she began to fill out and for the first time, looked healthy. We still had to unfold her every morning, but that deathly grey look was gone and she wasn't as stiff.

We took her to visit her aunt. When we dropped her off, her aunt took one look at her and commented on how fat she'd become. I couldn't believe it. There wasn't an ounce of fat on that child. Of course, this was the same woman who said she could only eat oatmeal and rice.

We eventually went to court because of Emma's family, not the mother, but the extended family. They wanted Emma in a native home. It was dismissed since the mom, the legal guardian was happy with the placement. Before her 12th birthday, Emma was moved and adopted.

Michelle was offered an opportunity to live with missionaries in Japan for three months. I took her to San Francisco the week before Christmas and off she flew. It was hard to let her go, but we both have such a heart for foreign missions that I was thrilled for her.

2000

Right after New Year's, we heard about Shelvin on the news. It was reported that a baby had been severely abused and was in the hospital in Anchorage. We contacted Lee, the woman who had been instrumental in placing Jenny with us. She gave us a little more detail and we told her we would be interested if he needed a placement. Things moved pretty quickly, and we were on our way to Anchorage. When we got there, we were told that the baby was ten weeks old. When he was brought in he wasn't breathing. He was revived, and they found him to have <u>RSV</u> as well as severe brain trauma. As they examined him and ran tests, they found that his trauma was from <u>shaken baby syndrome</u>. They also found evidence of broken ribs, skull fracture, broken arm, and broken leg. It was explained to me that the force needed to break bones in a newborn would be that of a grown man stomping on the child.

When the mother brought him in, she said he was accidentally dropped by a caregiver and quit breathing, and she shook him to try and wake him up. The tests showed that he had trauma on top of trauma. In other words, he suffered trauma from being shaken severely, which caused brain swelling, and then was shaken again. The police were called in, and an investigation ensued.

Lee took us to the hospital to meet Shelvin. As we walked down the hallway, I saw a beautiful baby in a swing in the doorway of his room. I remember thinking how cute he was as we passed on our way to the nurse's station. When we were led to Shelvin's room, I was delighted to find it was that same sweet baby. There was no visible damage, however, he was a much damaged little boy. Due to brain trauma, he could no longer suck and a g-tube was put in. He could not see due to <u>cortical blindness</u>. He had a hyperextension in his arms and was a little bundle of tension. He would not be comforted by touch or gentle caresses. When he was agitated, you simply had to put him down with no contact. When we got to the hospital, Shelvin's crib was full of beanie babies, balloons, and a picture of his parents. When we were getting ready to take him home, we went in and everything was gone. We asked about it and were told his parents had come in the night before and had taken everything. The nurses were pretty miffed since they were the ones who had brought in most of the toys. It gave a little insight into the mindset of the parents.

We spent a couple of days in Anchorage getting the details worked out, and then we took our little guy home.

After we had been home a few days, I noticed that Shelvin seemed to be tracking my face. I was so excited I called Dean at work to tell him Shelvin could see. I soon learned that with cortical blindness, the vision would come and go. It was frustrating because I so wanted him to improve, but he just didn't. Shelvin had to have physical therapy a couple of times a week due to his hyper extension. The therapist came to our house and showed me some techniques to help him loosen up as well. The poor little guy was in pain so much of the time. We did discover at the hot springs that putting him in really warm water was like watching a flower unfold. His little arms and legs would relax and he would literally sigh with relief. The heat was good for another issue that Shelvin had, <u>hypothermia</u>. The brain trauma affected his body's ability to regulate his temperature. Most of the time, he was just cool, but without any notice, his temperature would fall so low it wouldn't even register on the thermometer. We did a lot of body contact warming as well as heating pads and water bottles. It was just one of those things we came to check for and deal with as it came up.

One day after church, we went to the Grant's house with several church friends and Shelvin started getting cold. Bea knew what to do and got us a heating pad and we went to work getting him bundled and warmed up. One of the guests we had just recently met asked if this had happened a lot. Dean replied, "Well, he was white when we started." Shelvin's mother is an Alaskan native and his father is black. He is a beautiful mix of the two. He was stunned, but the rest of us just shook our heads. We were so used to Dean's humor .

I had planned to go to Japan with Keagan when it was time to get Michelle. The closer the time came, the more unruly he became. He was defiant, threatening, and completely uncooperative. Dean and I finally talked about it and decided I couldn't take the risk of him doing something while in another country. If he had one of his meltdowns, I don't know what I would have done. When we told Keagan, he acted like he was almost relieved. He told us that he knew I wasn't really going to take him. We tried to explain how our decision was based on his behavior, but he refused to accept any responsibility. It was amazing how good he got at making me feel guilty because of his behavior.

This wasn't the first time Keagan self-sabotaged. He would always act up before any holiday or vacation. It got to where we dreaded them rather than looking forward to them. No matter what we said, he was convinced it was because we didn't love him.

When we got home, we held a Welcome Home luau. Even though it was winter and our house was tiny, we didn't care. Dean's mom got us a side of pork from a butcher and we set up tables in the garage and games in the yard. It was awesome. About halfway through the party, the police arrived. They were asking about our luau and we explained about Michelle's homecoming. Then they asked about the pork. We told them that Mom had gotten it at the butchers. They wanted to see a receipt, but we didn't have one, she did. So we gave them her contact info. They finally explained that some meat had been stolen from a butcher shop, and a side of pork was one of the things taken. When someone saw us having a luau they turned us in as possible suspects. It was just a random coincidence.

We also had a surprise for Michelle. We got her a horse while she was gone. Ninia wasn't young and she'd definitely been through some neglect, but Michelle loved her. Ninia had been a pack horse and had her own ideas about how things were going to be. She set Keagan straight pretty much right away. He was hanging on her neck and she reached over him and bit him right on the bum. He was so mad. She also had her own ideas on where she wanted to go. Dean learned the hard way that when Ninia wants to go left, she's going left. Not only did she toss him, but she then continued on home and left him to walk.

We ended up leaving our church and started going to a non-denomination church where we met Pastor Darryl and Pauline. Pretty soon, I became the Children's Pastor and fell in love with teaching again. One of my favorites was the Pastor's son, Colton. Colton had a rough start in life and something in me was drawn to him. He became a part of our family and Keagan's little protégé. I would watch Keagan as he mentored Colton. He was so patient and tolerant with him. It was so different from the way he treated us.

The kids and I took a trip to see Lawana in Klawock and Papa in Ketchikan. After our short visit with Lawana, we headed to Ketchikan. When we got there, Shelvin started to run a fever and started vomiting. He couldn't keep anything down, so I took him to see Dr. J. He gave him some broad-spectrum antibiotics and took some cultures. Shelvin didn't improve at all, wasn't keeping anything down and was getting really dehydrated. When the cultures came back, we were all shocked. This baby, who only had formula through his Mic-Key, had food poisoning. And it came from poultry. They got him on the right antibiotics, and he finally started to improve. Lawana and I tried to figure out where this might have come from. Finally, she remembered that while she'd been thawing a turkey in the sink with cold water, Shelvin's bottles and tubes where drying on a towel beside the sink. Apparently, some turkey water must have splashed onto his things. It was unreal but the only possible explanation.

That summer, my 16 year-old niece Lacy came to Fairbanks to spend time with Grandma Margie and JB. We first met Lacy as a newborn in Wasilla. My sister-in-law had been contacted by a friend in Ketchikan who knew of a baby that would be up for adoption at birth. Plans were made, and she flew down to pick up her new baby girl. We were all so excited. She flew home and we saw her the next day at church. Lacy was an Alaskan native and had dark hair that stood straight up and the bluest eyes ever. As she grew she was like a walking happy face. She had this really deep voice and walked like a quarterback but she had a heart of gold. She was so adorable.

Their plan to adopt was unfortunately thwarted. M and P were not native, and even though the birth parents were in agreement, the native association fought them relentlessly until they just gave up.

I got to see Lacy pretty regularly during the first two years of her life since my sister-in-law watched Michelle for me while I worked. Lacy and Michelle are 18 months apart and were pretty close as toddlers.

When we moved to Ketchikan, we didn't see her except for an occasional vacation trip. So we were all pretty excited to get to spend time with her over the summer.

We found out that things were not great with Lacy. M had recently re-married, and Lacy and the new husband didn't get along. When Lacy was little, she had three older siblings who watched after her and babied her. As they grew up and moved away, it was just her and her mom, so it was understandable that there was tension. She spent a lot of time with us that summer and the end result was that she didn't want to return home. We talked with the family and it was agreed we would become her legal guardians. We went to work on getting her legally in our care. Since the adoption had never been finalized, M really couldn't give us guardianship, and I suppose we could have just raised her and not bothered, but it was important to Lacy and, therefore, important to us. We found out that to become her guardians, we would have to go back and get releases from the birth parents. We tracked them down and made contact. They were both under the impression she had been adopted years earlier and were understandably upset. It was emotionally difficult for Lacy who was trying to process all this as well as dealing with these "parents" who now wanted to be in her life. She handled it with a lot of maturity for a 16-year-old, and we supported her as best we could. She told her birth parents that this guardianship was what she wanted, and they both signed off. Once we had everything in place, we went to court and were appointed as her legal guardians. As we left the courthouse that day, I will never forget, Lacy came up to me and hugged me, and said, "I finally belong to someone."

We became Auntie Mom and Uncle Dad.

Once we were appointed guardians, the real fun began. Due to the non-adoption, Lacy didn't have a birth certificate or a social security number. We were finally able to get a birth certificate, but it was weird when they asked her what she wanted her name to be. She finally settled on the name she'd had all her life but did change her last name to her birth mother's. With that in hand, we tried for social security, but they wanted something with a picture. They sent us to DMV to get a state identification card. Unfortunately, they wouldn't issue it without a social security card. We went round and round until finally, after I lost it at the DMV, they agreed to give her the card if we signed affidavits that we had known her for her entire life and that she was, in fact, Lacy. We also agreed to bring the Social security card back once we had it. Once we had the ID, we were able to get the social security card. With these in place she began to work on her driver's license, and I took on the daunting task of applying for 16 years of back PFDs for her. It was a major pain, but once it was done she received around $20,000.00. So, well worth it in the end. She eventually used this money for school.

During that summer, Lacy re-dedicated her life to the Lord and really wanted to change her life. She had been making some pretty bad choices, one being that she basically failed 9th grade.

We got Lacy set up for home school and now I had three children I was teaching at home. The girls enjoyed working and being together, so they were pretty easy. Michelle was two years ahead of Lacy, so she was able to help her when she needed it. We were able to get Lacy caught up after the first year and she continued and graduated on time.

Keagan, on the other hand, did not do well. He hated homeschooling. Of course, he also hated public school, so we were at a loss about what to do. We put him back in public school after he absolutely refused to do any work at home. Fourth grade was not good. He had a teacher we both disliked, and with Keagan being Keagan, it was continual conflict all year long. At one point, the teacher accused Keagan of something that I knew wasn't true. When he told me, I said I would go to school and sort it out. Before I could get there, he asked for and received arbitration. Then, when it didn't go his way, he demanded that I fix it. I told him I was more than happy to get involved, but since he took it upon himself to deal with the issue, there was nothing I could do. He wasn't happy and the conflict continued.

Keagan started playing hockey in the house league. It took a bit for him to catch up with his skating abilities. Most of the kids had been playing since age four, so he was definitely behind. Once he got going, he was pretty good. Dean and I knew absolutely nothing about hockey, but we learned.

After a few weeks at home, we were visited by Shelvin's paternal grandmother. She was precious and adamant that her son was not responsible for Shelvin's injuries. We agreed to keep in touch, which we did for the remainder of Shelvin's life.

After returning home, we were told there was a problem with one of the native organizations. Apparently, Shelvin's mother contacted a regional native organization, not the one she was a member of, and told them the state had taken her baby and would not let her see him. She also made a point of telling them that we were white, which, of course, set them off. They contacted CPS and demanded that the mother have visitation, and they demanded to be told why the child had been taken. The case-worker told them that when they got a signed release from the mother to discuss the case with them, she would gladly explain the situation. The mother signed off, the case worker explained and that was the end of any native organization wanting anything to do with Shelvin. It always seemed weird that she did that since she had to know what they were going to be told.

Shelvin's father was in the army at the time of his injuries, and although he was a nice guy, he didn't seem to understand the severity of the situation. He got a dishonorable discharge and was arrested. I took Shelvin to see him in jail several months after he was placed with us. The dad was very grateful for the visit and for keeping in contact with his mother so he could get updates. But then he would ask me questions like, "Is he walking? Does he say Daddy?" and others. I explained several times that Shelvin did nothing except exist and this wasn't going to change. He seemed to understand then he would ask another question that left me shaking my head. I left there really frustrated and contacted his attorney, who had arranged the visit. I asked her why he hadn't been told about the severity of Shelvin's injuries. She assured me that every time she spoke to him, they had that same conversation. I don't know if he didn't understand or just refused to believe it. It broke my heart.

I had one visit with Shelvin's mother at the ARC in Anchorage. She seemed like a nice person but not really engaging. She was very pretty and very young.

When Shelvin came home with us, he could not suck. I would use my finger to press on his upper palate to stimulate the response and had some success. We tried a pacifier, but he couldn't keep it in, so we added elastic and hooked it around his ears, and he did really well. Eventually, we were told to try solid foods and we did. He never did manage to get enough down to make a difference but we did it anyway just for the therapeutic effect of introducing different textures and stimulation.

Shelvin's mother was taken into custody, sort of. She was placed in a halfway house while Shelvin's dad was in jail. Apparently, the state was stuck in the prosecution because they blamed each other for the abuse. It was a mess.

Lacy loved Shelvin and spent a lot of time holding him and loving on him. Because she was so beautiful, we would often observe, while we were out and about, teenage boys checking her out, looking for a way to approach. Dean was great; he would simply call out to her, "Hey, Lacy, come get your baby," and the boys would scatter.

About this time, Keagan had an epiphany. He figured that since others picked on him, he'd start being a bully and pick on them first. I assured him that if he started bullying other kids, I would show up every day with his little brain-damaged brother and follow him everywhere he went. It's pretty hard to be a bully with your mom right there. He knew I meant every word of it.

Finally, there was a hearing, and Shelvin's mom pleaded no contest to second-degree assault. I was allowed to give testimony on Shelvin's behalf.

I told them:

"This child will never live. He will never decide what to eat, what to wear, or what to do. His choices have been taken from him. He won't graduate from school, get married or have children. His future has been taken from him. His life was taken from him in a brutal manner, and no one is paying for it.

The judge thanked me for my comments and then proceeded to tell Shelvin's mother, "I want you to know how proud I am of you, that while you were incarcerated you got your GED. I also know that what happened was a terrible accident that will never be repeated." He gave her time served and wished her well.

The dad pleaded no contest to child endangerment. Once he did his time, he was released and went home. I never heard from or saw either of them again.

It took Shelvin about nine months to get to the place where he would be comforted by touch, but it was never gentle touch, it had to be firm, or it would actually stress him. Several times at church, women would see me with him and ask to hold him. I didn't mind, but I knew he'd be back very soon because they just couldn't help themselves. Their soft nurturing caresses would stress him, and he'd start crying.

I started using a heavy quilt with Shelvin and it made a huge difference in his sleep. It gave him enough assurance that he could relax and sleep.

Shelvin had several bouts of pneumonia, which isn't uncommon for kids who aren't mobile. We would end up in the hospital for a few days where he got antibiotics and oxygen. The doctors always had a horrible time getting an IV into Shelvin. They told me his veins rolled. The best time we ever had was with a retired army medic who got it on the first shot. I wish I could have requested him every time.

2001

The year Michelle graduated, she got the opportunity to go to Africa. Her little missionary heart never thought twice about missing her graduation. She went with a group from the church and had a wonderful time. She came back with a distaste for American materialism and a renewed passion for missions.

After her return, Michelle decided to move to Oregon and go to college in The Dalles. Uncle Vince had offered her a place to stay, so she was off. As it got close to school time, she changed her mind and decided to go to Master's Commission in Marysville, Washington. We were pretty happy with her decision. I went down and helped her move to Washington. Master's Commission provides homes for their students, so Michelle lived with a church family in the area. Once she was settled, I headed back home and left her in the care of others. She really enjoyed the opportunities she had while in school. She got to preach, do dance and drama, visit Ukraine, and really focus on God. She ended up staying for almost three years.

I got a phone call from Michelle one evening after church. During the service, a woman came up to her and told her she had a word for her. The woman then went on to tell her that God wanted her to know that he was releasing her from the fear that she'd been holding on to for years. She also said that Michelle had been attacked as a young child because the enemy saw her potential and wanted to stop her from being used by God. The minute she heard it, she was her old self again. I was so relieved when she told me about the encounter. My girl was back.

As Lacy finished up high school, she was given an opportunity to go to several countries across Europe with People to People. She was so excited since she'd traveled very little. As we prepared for her trip and her following graduation, it dawned on me that I was moving into an empty nest situation. I'd still have my little angry bird and my broken bird but no girls to have fun with.

2003

When Lacy graduated, she decided to move to Texas with her friend Gina. We were concerned because she could be terribly naïve. It wasn't long until we got the phone call. She was pregnant. I was so sad for her. I tried to talk her into coming home for a bit, but she refused. She wanted to marry her boyfriend, Andy. I wasn't against him but I wanted her to take some time before she rushed into it. I assured her that we were here for her whatever she decided to do. I made sure she knew that her baby was a precious gift from God, and although it wasn't the circumstances we would have hoped for, we were excited about the baby.

Our church was sending a team to Africa on a mission trip, and I was excited to go. My time in Africa was pretty amazing. I went on a safari and ministered at a prison. I visited an orphanage and made some amazing friends.

When Keagan was 12, he came home one day with a video game, jewelry and money. When I asked him about it, he told me it was from a friend. Later that evening, as we headed out to eat, we passed police at a neighbor's house. When we got home, the Alaska State Troopers showed up at our door. They asked to talk to Keagan. They questioned him about a break-in and vandalism at a neighbor's house. I was shocked. The Troopers asked about specific items: games, money, jewelry and guns.

We were told the house and car were shot up. Guns were thrown in the slough. Lots of destruction and along with the stolen items. We were told to get a lawyer on retainer as he and his friend were looking at felony charges. The boys' excuse was that it was a run-down little shack and the back door was open. They thought no one lived there.

Both families ended up paying 3-4k in restitution and the boys were required to work off part of it. Unfortunately, no charges were ever filed, and after a few weeks, Keagan was done with it. He asked me to buy him something and I said no. When he asked why I just looked at him and then asked, "Are you for real?" He blew up and said, "Am I going to hear about this for the rest of my life?" I thought of all the ways we could have used $4,000.00 and said, "Yes!"

In November, Lacy got married and she had a little boy.

When Keagan hit Jr. High, his behavior at school began to be a real problem. He was sent out of class for being disruptive and disrespectful. He talked to the school counselor and had her convinced that I was the problem. He skipped over 40 days of school. When he would refuse to go, I would call the school, identify myself and say that he was not coming. I said I was aware of his absence but did not excuse it. They never responded. I finally contacted them and

I was told that it was my responsibility to get him to school. I explained that I could not physically force him, and he became violent when I tried.

I was told that the only thing they could do was arrest me. I said I was okay with that as long as they did it when Keagan was there so he would see the consequences of his actions. They did nothing. When he failed pretty much everything, they enrolled him in summer school for six weeks. He attended most days and was promoted to High School.

Keagan and I had frequent arguments that usually resolved themselves without too much family disruption. On one occasion it just kept escalating so I left the room. I went into my bedroom to calm down. Keagan followed me and continued to argue. I left the house and got into my car. I thought a drive would help me calm down. As I pulled out of the driveway, Keagan forced himself into the car. He was relentless and would not back down. As I neared our church, I completely lost it and told him I hated him. I had intended to say I hated the way he was acting, but there it was. I apologized, but he wouldn't listen. It was as if he was glad that I'd finally said out loud what he'd always believed to be true. I pulled over on the shoulder and got out of the car. As I stood there trying to figure out what to do, Dean pulled up behind me. He was heading home and saw me on the side of the road. I briefly explained what had happened, then I headed to the church. I found Pastor Darryl, and we had a long talk. He felt sure that Keagan would accept my apology once he calmed down, and everything would be okay. I wasn't sure, but even if he forgave me, how was I ever going to forgive myself? I loved that boy more than he could possibly know, and in that moment, when he needed my assurance, I had failed him.

2004

Thanks to No Child Left Behind, it was decided that Shelvin needed to go to school. I understood the reasoning behind the policy but Shelvin was not going to benefit from going to school. He had an

EEG to check for brain activity. The first time they did it while he was asleep. Afterwards they decided to do one while he was awake. After the second one, I was told there was so little happening in his brain that he was, for all intents and purposes, brain-dead. The technician told me that she doubted me when I told her he did have awake times.

The only real benefit from sending Shelvin to school was that his therapy and chair maintenance could happen there. The bad part was all the germs and illnesses he was exposed to. His health was precarious at best and now he was being exposed daily to every type of germ or bacteria around.

We were pleasantly surprised when we found out his teacher was the mom of Ben, Adam and Sam, the boys we'd done respite for.

Keagan and I got into an argument that turned physical. When Dean saw him attack me, he tried to intervene, and Keagan got physical with him. It was really scary. Dean was usually the one that could help him calm down, but not this time. It escalated to him pushing Dean aside and storming out of the house. I called our friends, the Grants, who had several strong men in the family, and asked if a couple of the guys could come over. Before they arrived, I saw our car leave the driveway. I called the police and told them my 15-year-old sons just drove away in my car without permission or license. Keagan returned shortly after the police arrived. They took him into his room and had a long talk with him. When they left, they told us they wouldn't bring charges but warned Keagan that they had better not get another call to the house. He stayed in his room the rest of the evening. The next day, he was back to normal.

As Shelvin grew, it became more of an effort to maneuver him. We had a kiddie kart, a wheelchair/stroller combo unit. We used a bath chair for him and he had to be in a car seat for travel. Around the house, we mostly carried him. His caseworker, who was so wonderful, talked to us about home modifications that would be needed as Shelvin grew. We talked about a wheelchair van, a rail system to move him from room to room, walk-in shower, ramps, wider doors, and all sorts of modifications. We were told that there was going to be a lawsuit and if they won, Shelvin would have money that would pay for these improvements.

The lawsuit was based on medical malpractice. His mother had taken Shelvin into the native clinic shortly before he was hospitalized and said there was something wrong with his eyes. The doctor, after doing an examination, suspected abuse and ordered a "baby gram," which is code for doing a full body scan because abuse is suspected. The x-ray was done and when it was read the doctor was told it was fine. She sent Shelvin home with eye drops. Later the x-ray was looked at and it showed several fractures. How sad it was that if it had been read correctly, or at all, Shelvin would have been taken into protective custody before the additional incidents of abuse. He could have still had a life. Because the native hospital is financed by the federal government the suit was against them.

Keagan hit puberty, and all of a sudden, there were girls. I really didn't like him moving in and out of these relationships, but I tried to encourage him to be a gentleman and treat them right. As these relationships ran their course, I tried not to get caught up in the drama, but sometimes you just can't help it. One of the girls was really nice, but super quiet around us, so we didn't know her well. I thought it was just her nature, but it turned out she was fighting her own demons. She attempted suicide, and since both families attended the same church, everyone knew about it. One of the youth leaders made the assumption that because Keagan was her boyfriend, he must be the cause. Keagan had a reputation as a troublemaker around the church, and he probably deserved it, but not everything was his fault. The leader took Keagan aside and ripped into him something fierce, blaming him for potentially ruining this girl's life. For once, Keagan didn't respond in kind but simply walked away. He knew the truth about the situation, and this man didn't. Instead of defending himself and thereby revealing confidences, he kept quiet. When this mama bear heard about it, I was livid. I couldn't believe this grown man thought he had the right to berate my under-age son without even talking to us. After I calmed down, I had a talk with the leader. He agreed he was out of line and apologized. That was all well and good, but my real take-away was the maturity I saw in Keagan. It gave me hope for his future.

I went to Africa again and it was every bit as magical as the first time. I got to visit an orphanage for children with Aids. One of the little girls there wanted me to pick her up and I was told not to because of her condition. I didn't care. I reached out and grabbed hold of her and gave her a big hug. I don't understand how others can't see it, but children aren't supposed to suffer, and when they do, we should do whatever we can to give comfort. We painted a mural at another orphanage and I did an object lesson with crafts for the older kids. I loved being around those kids and could seriously see myself being there full-time in the future.

2005

We lost Papa right after the New Year. We had planned to go visit him in January, but we didn't make it in time. Dean and I went back to Ketchikan to help sort things out along with his brother and sister. It was heart-wrenching. Papa had been such a huge supporter of our odd little family. We still miss him to this day.

Shelvin began to have lung issues. We had to suction him when he had problems breathing. This was a new skill for me to learn, and I never really got comfortable with it. I was always nervous about getting it in the right place.

Shelvin wasn't feeling well, so I took him to the doctor. She detected some noise in his lungs, and although it didn't sound bad, she felt that with his history, he should be admitted to the hospital for a few days. Once again, we checked in, Shelvin got poked and they eventually got a questionable IV in his foot. He was there a couple of days, but his oxygen saturation didn't improve. He got worse and was moved to ICU and put on a ventilator. The doctors were giving him seriously strong antibiotics and told me they were concerned that if his IV blew, the medicine would actually eat his skin, so they needed to get another line in. They decided to operate and put a line in his jugular vein. I spoke to CPS and requested that they issue a DNR order and they refused. They told me when he was placed with us that if his health deteriorated to the point he was on life support, they would let him die. Now, they were telling me that every measure to save his life was to be used. I was furious. I was so afraid he would end up in a home on a ventilator. As I sat by his bed, listening to music and holding his hand, I told him it was okay. That if he needed to die to get peace, it was okay.

They took Shelvin to the OR and I headed out to the waiting room. The procedure was supposed to take 45 minutes to an hour. When an hour came and no word, I started to get concerned. At 1 hour 15 minutes, I heard the code and knew it was Shelvin. The nurse came into the waiting room and told me I needed to go to the OR. Per hospital procedure, they dressed me in scrubs and put me in a wheelchair and took me down. When I got there, I saw his little body on the table. The nurse above his head was using a bag to breathe for him. The surgeon was performing CPR and his neck wound was still open. They took me to his side, looked at me, and asked, "What do you want us to do?" I said, "I want you to let him go." They immediately removed their hands and stood by as Shelvin passed away. I held his hand and watched him go. Another nurse in the room asked me if I wanted her to call anyone. I gave her my Pastor's name and number and she called him.

Pastor Darryl later recalled getting that phone call. The nurse told him that he needed to come to the hospital as Mrs. Stackhouse's son had just died and I was requesting him to come. He said he'd be right there and hung up. Then he turned to Pauline, his wife, and said, "Who is Mrs. Stackhouse? Her son just died, and she wants me to come." Pauline reminded him that Stackhouse was Shelvin's last name and it was me.

They took me back upstairs, and I called Dean and the Grants and waited. They eventually brought him up to me and I held him. Because of the tightness of Shelvin's muscles his little fingers would still tighten when his hand was moved and I put my finger in his hand and his muscles made it feel like he was holding on.

Eventually, it was time to go but I couldn't just leave him there until he was picked up by the funeral home. That's when his nurse came in and promised me he would not leave Shelvin's side until the funeral home came for him. The professionalism in the ICU gave me such peace and assurance as they cared for Shelvin. I could not have asked for anything more.

We won the lawsuit and Shelvin was awarded 1.25 million. The terms of the settlement were that the money could be used for anything Shelvin needed, but when he died, anything remaining reverted back to the government. The news came just days before he was hospitalized yet again for pneumonia. He died 10 days after receiving the settlement, and the only thing that was paid for out of it was his funeral.

When we went to the funeral home and made plans for his burial I was shocked to see the size of caskets they wanted us to choose from. I kept thinking he wasn't that big and needed a smaller one, but when I saw him in it, he actually fit. The casket was white and we put his blanket and some of his favorite things inside with him.

When I first saw Shelvin at the funeral, I was a little shocked by his appearance. I had never seen anyone who'd been autopsied before and it was obvious that things had been done to him. His eyes and mouth were glued shut, his chest felt like a blanket was under his shirt. He was wearing his African shirt that I brought him back from Uganda and his knitted cap. I remember arranging his little afro until he looked just right.

Michelle came home for the funeral and helped with a lot of the planning. She also took pictures of the ceremony, but unfortunately these were lost in a house fire years later.

I was determined it would not be a somber occasion. We had the boys in the church, including Keagan, act as pall bearers while dressed in bright Hawaiian shirts. One of my former Children's church kids wrote and sang a song about Shelvin. Pastor Darryl did an amazing job of reminding us that Shelvin was going home. It was hard when they came to close the lid. There's something final about shutting and locking the top of the casket. At the conclusion of the service, we released biodegradable balloons out in the beautiful sunshine. Our little boy was finally free.

Because Shelvin died on St. Patrick's Day, he could not be buried right away. Fairbanks has permafrost, and they couldn't dig up the ground until it thawed. His body would be stored at the funeral home until summer, then we would have his burial.

A couple of weeks after Shelvin's death, I had a dream. Now before I share it, I want you to know I am not someone who gets visions and if someone else told me this story, I would be terribly skeptical, so it's okay if you think it's a little weird. I'm just going to relate what happened. In my dream, I was looking down on the OR where Shelvin died. I could see him on the operating table, the surgeon beside him, and the nurse holding the bag above his head. I was in the wheelchair beside him but none of us were moving. Then I saw Shelvin with his full afro, dressed in white, walking alongside someone that I could only see from the waist down with his hand clutched in Shelvin's. Shelvin looked down on the OR scene, looked up, and said, "Will she hurt? To which the voice replied, "Yes, she will." Shelvin looked down again and asked, "Will she be all right?" The voice answered "Yes, she will." When I woke up, an incredible heaviness was lifted and I was able to grieve without being completely overwhelmed. It wasn't that Shelvin had anything to really live for. His life had been taken years before, but he left such a hole in our daily lives. His sweet presence and our own loss was what we were really mourning. But now I knew without a doubt that he was whole, he was safe, and he was loved.

Shortly after Shelvin died, Michelle decided to leave Master's Commission and came home. She started helping out around the church and it was fun to have her around while I was working. It wasn't long until Thor followed her to North Pole. They had been at MC together and had become close. Thor was certain that he and Michelle were meant to be together and Michelle let him convince her. Thor was a really nice guy but he'd lived a hard life before going to Master's Commission. He took offense at the smallest things and his anger was intense. We all found ourselves walking on eggshells around him.

He asked Dean for permission to marry her and Dean said, "No." It wasn't a "you must be kidding" no, just a "this is happening way too fast" no. Thor proposed that night. So, we were not a little concerned. Thor was a great guy and had a heart for ministry, but they were not suited to each other. Michelle didn't tell anyone they were engaged. I tried to point out our concerns but she just got mad. I knew if she was pushed she'd marry him to prove her point. So, I talked to Pastor Darryl and he told me not to worry. He had his own plans for Michelle. First, he talked to them both and pointed out that all couples come into a relationship with baggage and they both had theirs. However, while Michelle was lugging her suitcase, Thor was coming in with a U-Haul.

Pastor Darryl offered Michelle a chance to spend three months in Uganda with a missionary family. She was thrilled. Thor was not. I told Michelle if she'd go and use that time apart to make sure this was what she wanted, I would support whatever decision she made. She agreed.

After she'd been in Africa for about a month, she got in touch. She'd met someone and actually kissed him. She was really confused and had already told Thor. She wanted to put their engagement on hold until she came home and they could talk about it. He was livid and told everyone who would listen that Michelle had cheated on him. He also refused to break their engagement and wanted her to come home now.

Along with Ben, Adam and Sam, we started doing weekly respite for a little guy named Tony. Tony was born with arthrogryposis. His arm and leg joints were stiff and the limbs themselves were floppy. He had no control over them. His spine was so bent that he literally rested his head on his butt. We were told that while pregnant, Annie had lost her amniotic fluid. She either didn't realize it or didn't know it was a problem so she never sought care. So Tony's little body was stuck and not allowed to develop properly.

When we met Annie, we were told she'd just lost a baby girl and needed some help. Tony took a lot of work and she also had a very active four-year-old as well. We agreed to take him on the weekends so she could have a break. Tony needed lots of PT to keep him limber, but otherwise, it was g-tube feedings and diaper changes. As he got older, he needed glasses and eventually had surgery on his feet.

We went to pick him up the weekend he got his casts off and were surprised he hadn't been bathed. When we removed his AFO's there was dead skin all over his legs. Most weekends, we started him out with a bath because Annie liked to keep him super oily with really strong smelling lotions. This weekend he had to be bathed because all that dead skin under his cast was still there and stunk something terrible.

In June, when the weather warmed up, we were finally able to bury Shelvin. Keagan and I arrived early and they brought his casket out. It was unlocked and I wanted to open it and see him one more time but I just couldn't. I knew his remains had been refrigerated and he would look the same but I just couldn't do it. I don't remember who all came to the service, but there weren't many of us. He was laid to rest and a short while later the headstone was in place. I sent a picture of his headstone to his grandmother and let her know where he was buried. That was the last communication I had with her.

I used to go up and leave flowers for him, and one time I found a flower in his vase. I was surprised and couldn't figure out who left it since very few people knew where he was buried. I asked a couple of people about it but no one seemed to know anything. This happened several more times, and I finally mentioned it to my pastor. Darryl told me it was his precious mother. Apparently, his father's grave is nearby, and every time she took flowers to his gravesite, she would pull out one flower and put it in Shelvin's vase. I was so moved I began to reciprocate. It somehow made it easier to visit, knowing I could bless someone else as well.

When Michelle did come home, she and Thor finally got together and talked it through. The engagement was off.

She and Kirk, the man she'd met in Africa, spent the following months figuring out how they felt about each other. In December, with Dean's permission they got engaged.

As Keagan moved into high school, his behavior didn't improve. He spent more time with the janitor than in class. The only class he really got something out of was JROTC. His private counselor said he needed one on one tutoring and an IEP. The school disagreed. They had me fill out all kinds of forms, spoke to his teachers, had Keagan take tests, and talked to us. They came to the conclusion that I was the problem, he was fine.

2006

In April, we went to Oregon for Michelle's wedding. It was such a beautiful time. We were blessed to have so many of our friends there. Pastor Darryl came down and did a joint ceremony with Kirk's pastor, Pastor Craig.

On our way home, we dropped Keagan off in Wrangell at a camp for kids with behavior issues. When we picked him up six weeks later, he seemed much more agreeable and we were hopeful. Since the violence wasn't near as much and we were somewhat able to talk to

Keagan, we decided to quit counseling. We'd been taking him for seven years and really made very little progress. I asked one counselor why all his counseling hadn't made much of a difference and he told me there is no cure for RAD. They had only been seeing Keagan so they could give me advice on how to cope with his behavior.

When we agreed to quit counseling and allow him a choice about his medication, it made a huge difference. We told him he didn't have to take it but he could not use it as an excuse for bad behavior. He began to figure out how to express himself in acceptable ways. Hockey was a huge outlet for him as well as hunting and riding his quads.

Keagan didn't go back to school. There really wasn't any point. We signed him up for on-line school but he wasn't interested. We tried to get him into an alternative school but they wouldn't take him. I spoke to the Superintendent and pleaded for help. He basically said that if Keagan couldn't function in school it was my problem. So at 15, Keagan quit school and began to work on his GED. Keagan was lacking when it came to writing essays, so we went into the center where they help you so you can pass the GED. For some reason, this woman would give Keagan instructions, then after he re-wrote the paper, would point out additional issues. After four re-writes and she was still finding fault Keagan was done and I couldn't really blame him. So, no GED. Eventually, I compiled my own GED for homeschooling. He took my test and I issued him a home school diploma. Done and done.

Tony got a kiddie kart, a small child's wheelchair. With most kids, it was always easier with a wheelchair, but with Tony, it was such a pain to get him in it because of how his spine was bent that we usually just carried him around.

I took a job assisting the preschool teacher at the local Christian school. It was fun, and I really enjoyed working with the kids. The parents were another story, and when the year was done, so was I.

2007

I got a position as a roving lunch lady. That was fun and led to a permanent position. I liked being a lunch lady a lot. It gave me opportunities to be around kids and to keep busy.

As Tony got older, we ended up getting more involved with the medical side of his care. We took him to PT and, at his mom's request, would go with her to the doctor or hospital. Annie had a hard time understanding what the doctor was telling her a lot of the time and so she relied on Dean and me to break it down for her.

2008

When it came tax time, Bea asked me to consider taking the H & R Block class at the office where she worked. She always got frustrated with me at tax time. I found taxes so overwhelming that I always took my documents to her at the last minute. She thought if I took the class, I could at least do my own taxes and, I wouldn't be so anxious over them. As it turned out, I liked doing taxes once I knew how and was offered a job at H&R Block. I started working for them starting mid-January through April. I made good money and I had the rest of the year to myself. It was hard work and we worked long days. Dean took on most of the family responsibilities during tax time since I usually came home wiped out. I continued to work the tax season each year until I moved.

2009

When Tony got older, we started seeing more neglect and became concerned. We started keeping him longer and Annie began to rely on us more and more. We wanted to support her, but our first priority was always going to be Tony.

One weekend Dean and I were sitting beside Tony on the couch and he rolled onto his side and continued to roll off the sofa. He hit his mouth and his gum bled a bit. We told Annie what happened, and we thought that was that. A few days later, she called and said his tooth was black and wanted to know what had happened. We told her it was probably from the fall and she acted like we hadn't told her about it. I felt bad about the tooth but it was just something that happened.

We continued to watch him and saw more signs of neglect. He was sunburned from being left in the car all day while she worked with her dad. He was always dirty and we could tell he wasn't getting the PT because his spine was tighter than it had been.

2011

Finally, it all came to a head one weekend. After we picked him up, we noticed he was pretty lethargic. We fed him when we got home and I went to change him before bed. His diaper was completely dry. The next morning I went to change him and it was completely dry. I fed him breakfast and then later lunch, but still no wet diaper. He finally had a minimally wet diaper before bed that night. I was really concerned. I took him to the doctor the next day and told her what was going on. She was livid. She filed a complaint with CPS and scolded me for not bringing him in the previous day. She figured he hadn't been fed in days.

Annie called us and asked us to take Tony. She was a bit hysterical and said she couldn't take care of him anymore. I assumed she wanted us to take him for good, so we went in and got him and started making arrangements to have him full-time. After a week, she called and wanted to know when we were bringing him home. We were so confused.

After the doctor's complaint finally made its way back to Annie, she made accusations against us. She accused us of burning Tony with cigarettes and being neglectful. We ended up having a meeting with his caseworker and the director of that agency along with Annie and her boyfriend. I told her the spots were mosquito bites and we'd already explained how he fell. She basically said since we'd reported her, she reported us. I was shocked when she went on to ask us when we were taking Tony again. I told her we would only take him if it were a full-time permanent placement. We felt like that was the only way we could be sure he was going to have his needs met. Dean and I agreed that we couldn't continue to spend our weekends trying to make up for four days of neglect. That wasn't what she wanted. She wanted us to be at her beck and call 24/7 and we weren't willing to do that any longer. We told her we were done and left the meeting.

Keagan, now 19, decided to move to Oregon. He was working as a car salesman for a while, but decided that wasn't for him. He then enrolled in a forestry training program, but that wasn't for him either. He eventually decided to return to North Pole.

Annie called about a month after the meeting to thank me for the birthday gift I sent to Tony. She then asked if we would watch Tony. I told her no and that was the last time we heard from her.

Michelle got pregnant not long after getting married and I was over the moon. My grandson was born the following year and all I wanted to do was be around him. He was followed by two precious granddaughters that I hated being apart from. I spent as much time as I could in Oregon to be around them.

2012

My last year of doing taxes, I had a man come in to file his return. He began to give me information about his dependents, and I recognized the names. I asked him if his son Tony was our Tony and he said he was. Since I had never met Tony's father, it completely took me off guard. I told him who I was and asked how Tony was doing. He told me he'd died earlier that year. I was shocked. I eventually got control of myself and finished his taxes. After he left, I went to Bea's office and told her about Tony. I was still with her when Tony's dad came back. He'd gone home and got one of the funeral pamphlets from the service for me. It was such a kind thing to do.

Dean got a job out of Barrow. He works six weeks on and two weeks off. We decided that since he wouldn't be home anyway, I could move to Oregon permanently. When he was not working, one of us would fly to where the other one was.

I got an apartment not far from Michelle and got to see my grands as much as I wanted. They brought so much joy to me. I felt like my heart was literally overflowing.

I got a call from Keagan. He and his friend had done something incredibly stupid. They stole a piece of expensive equipment from the base PX. They got caught, returned the equipment, and paid restitution to the PX. He hadn't told me about it at the time because he believed it was resolved, but now the state of Alaska decided to bring charges against them, and he was going to court. Dean and I refused to get him a lawyer, so he went with the public defender. When he got to court, he admitted what he'd done and accepted the punishment. He did community service, paid more fines, and took a college course, per the judge's order.

Kirk's sister, Kara, got into some trouble and her daughter needed a placement, so once again, I got licensed. Kelsey was a toddler when she was first placed with me. She ended up staying with me several times, but every time she went back to Kara. Each time she came back, it was harder and harder to get her stable. She was witness to a lot of dysfunction, and that was what she considered normal. When she was with me, she had things like regular meals and consistent bedtimes, and she fought me tooth and nail. Finally, after a few years of watching her go back and forth, I had to be done. Kelsey was my last foster child.

2013

Michelle had one more surprise for me, and I got another granddaughter.

2014

One day Keagan came across a name at his place of employment that he recognized. It was his birth father who now lived in Fairbanks. He asked a co-worker about him and eventually contacted him. The man was full of stories about how he'd tried to find him and hoped they'd meet some day. After they talked for a bit and he saw Keagan wasn't the kind of man he expected him to be, he told him about another man his birth mom had dated. He felt like maybe he was Keagan's birth father. He asked him to do a DNA test. Keagan agreed and left, expecting to hear from him. Keagan and I talked about it, and he was a little disappointed but pretty accepting. He said he's totally fine with the dad he has. We haven't heard anything from the birth father to date.

2015

Dean and I got a phone call from Keagan. He was considering having a friend in need come stay with him and Leslie, his girlfriend, until she got back on her feet. He wanted to make sure we were okay with it since he lives in our house. I was overwhelmed. Keagan, the narcissist, was willing to inconvenience himself for someone else's well-being. I started crying and told him how proud I was of him. His response was, "Well, I had really good parents."

2020

I now live in Texas, surrounded by family. Dean will be retiring soon, and we're looking forward to our sunset years. The grands are growing up fast and we're blessed to have good relationships with them.

I am still involved with children. I work with Pastor Darry's organization, My360Project, a faith-based ministry that provides shoes for children around the world, as well as providing jobs and promoting mission trips. I am also involved with Royal Family Kids, a ministry that runs summer camps and mentoring programs for children in foster care. Both of these enable me to still make a difference in the lives of children.

There have been many people over the years who try to make us out like super saints or something. Let me just say here and now, we are not and never were. We are as fallible as anyone else. We just knew what we were called to do, and when opportunities came up, we did it. We also rely heavily on God's grace and strength. Every child we've cared for came from him and we were simply allowed to love and care for them for a time.

Michelle and Kirk are happily raising their kids and running their own businesses. They are still planning on missionary work when the grands are a little older.

Keagan worked through his issues and became an amazing young man that I couldn't be prouder of. He and I have a great relationship and look forward to our visits with each other. He and Leslie just celebrated two years of marriage. They are living up north, still enjoying the wilds of Alaska.

Lacy is living in Texas with her husband. From what I gather from social media she is doing well. Unfortunately, we are no longer in communication. I wish it was different, but sometimes you just can't fix things.

Ben lost his life to drugs. Adam joined the military and last I heard is doing well. Sam was working towards his GED last time I saw him.

Jacob, Jenny, Shelvin and Tony are all with God.

Then there are the others;

The native baby that was sexually molested by her grandfather. CPS thought we didn't need to know that, so she was traumatized every time Dean tried to change her diaper.

The little girl with CP and microcephaly who had a penchant for biting people. She would lunge sideways while in her chair and bite anyone within reach. She died of aspiration.

The nine-month-old who was left in her baby seat so much that her head was flat in the back. She was left in front of a space heater until her feet burned through to the bones.

The little girl who brought measles into my home because her parents didn't get her immunized.

The kids whose mother was in an accident. When the home was inspected before returning the children, they found no furniture, just jars of urine on every surface.

The five-year-old who had been left in charge of her little brother while her mother partied. She tried to kill herself three times after being re-united with her mother.

The little girl that we had to threaten to abandon at the police station before her caseworker would talk to us.

The 16-year-old that suffocated her newborn inside her parka while riding with her boyfriend on his snow machine. After she was revived, she lost her vision, her hearing and her ability to eat. She was inconsolable and whined constantly. She lived for about a year.

The kids whose mother was in the hospital. They were a wild and crazy bunch who got into everything. We found one little guy trying to squeeze more eggs out of the chickens.

All of these and more were our children for a time

Epilogue

Broken children can be broken in body, soul and spirit. Sometimes the cause is truly no one's fault, but still, children are hurt. A good friend's father was unwell for a long time and her mother was his primary caregiver. The outcome was brokenness in the kids whose needs were put aside to some degree so the father's more urgent needs could be met.

Some are broken due to addictions. When parents put their desires above the child's needs, the child experiences brokenness. Some kids are born addicted or with life-long disabilities because of addictions. Some are basically abandoned as their parents pursue their drug of choice.

Some, like my son, are broken by real or perceived rejection. When a child is or believes themselves to be rejected, something breaks inside them. The belief that there must be something wrong with a child if their own parent doesn't want them can be devastating.

There is verbal abuse that tears down the child in his own mind.

There is sexual abuse that brings shame and self-hatred. Horrible on its own, but so much more of a betrayal when it's a parent or family member. Or when the parents choose not to believe them when a child bravely tries to get help.

There is physical abuse that can cause irreparable damage to an infant and unspeakable terror for any child.

Apathy is possibly one of the most overlooked forms of abuse. I have had grown-ups tell me their parents didn't even care enough to get mad at them. They were unimportant in their own families.

All forms of abuse bring brokenness, but not everyone responds the same. It's impossible to know which kids will be able to use those experiences to become overcomers and which will allow themselves to become lifelong victims.

Every child I have encountered in the system is broken to some degree. No matter how good your intentions are, a foster home is a major adjustment for these kids. When they come to us they are grieving the loss of parents, siblings, home, neighborhood, school, friends, pets, possessions, and everything they are familiar with. They also give up on hopes and dreams. In other words, they have just lost every piece of their foundation. Even if it's a bad home situation, at least it's known.

So when these children show up at your door with a plastic trash bag in tow, they are broken. They will act out, they will horde, they will be disruptive, they will be defiant, and they will test you to the tips of your toes because they are broken.

Many people have asked me about foster care. They are usually thinking about signing up or getting involved in one way or the other. My first instinct is to tell them to run! Seriously, we have been hurt, lied to, lied about, and accused of horrible things by parents and caseworkers. We thought we would be appreciated and applauded for opening our home to children going through difficulties. If that's what you think, you do not need to be a foster parent. If, however, you know this is what you're supposed to do and aren't scared away by the likelihood of unpleasantness, then I applaud you. I don't have a lot of faith in the foster care system, but it's all we've got and what we have to work with. My greatest joy in life has been knowing that children's lives were made a little better by me doing my thing. If I have planted a seed of hope, shown a glimmer of how loved they are by their Father, been a place of refuge, or just given them a reason to smile then it was worth it and I would do it all again for my kids.

Jacob, by Aunt Lawana McGuffey

I had heard that the McFarland's had a child with shocking special needs. We were new to the area, and well-meaning members of our small community always mentioned Jacob when they saw our infant son with severe dwarfism. People were sure the McFarland's, with their broken boy and quirky adults, would be a perfect friendship – fit for us quirky McGuffeys and our broken baby.

I immediately poised myself to dislike them. (I didn't think people appreciated us and our individuality quite enough and hated being typecast as "just like" some family I didn't know).

At the same time, on the other end of the match-making grapevine, Kelly was also steeling her heart to dislike me!

Then…we met. All the descriptions had not prepared me for Jacob! He appeared not to be human. The throw-of-the-dice randomness of his facial features didn't coincide with the even bilateral numbers a human face required. His head shaped like a giant piece of candy corn did not seem compatible with human life. Though I knew he was a person, my brain could not construct people-ness from the jumble of misshapen features I saw. Indeed, as was a common response from others, my brain said "puppet."

I can't say that Kelly and I came down from our prejudicial high horses to an instant friendship. Rather we were swept up in a tide of similar circumstances, a mutual love for God and the gregarious hospitality that defines Kelly's husband Dean, Kelly and I, as well. Our families were tossed together like sand in a breaking wave and redeposited as family, never to be sorted out. We were and are family…the McFamily.

Because of Jacob, there was room for everyone. Though they were undoubtedly large before, I suspect Jacob enlarged the McFarlands. He taught them how to love more perfectly to give and give boatloads of time, love and care to a little guy who appeared to have little to give in return.

We were privileged to witness the giving back that Jacob did when we were invited to leave our stuffy apartment for their seaside home. These enchanted months together changed us forever!

Jacob was the hub. The rest of the family came and went to school, to work, and home again. Everyone entered the heart of the home through the Jacob-door. Bits of tube feeding, diaper changing, and personal care were linked together with smacky kisses, tickles and loud one-sided greetings. "Hey Jacob!", "Whatcha doing' buddy?" We never tired of watching Jacob show off his repertoire of things he was never supposed to be able to do. We delighted in his sloth-like slo-mo crawling and play. We loved the Jak-ish way he did impersonations. For instance, he held one misshapen little fist where his nose could have been when asked to do "Jimmy Durante."

We all worked and played with Jacob on our laps or on our hips. In everything, Jacob was included. Life was slowed, widened and stretched to envelop this odd little boy with the broken puppet face. At the same time, easy love, grace and acceptance of brokenness encompassed us all. At Jacob's side, we soaked up unconditional love as we had never known it before.

Shelvin, by Aunt Lawana McGuffey

The first time I saw Shelvin, I was touched by his apparent perfection. He was such a beautiful smooth brown with glossy hair. I wasn't in the home with Shelvin, so I missed some stages. In the beginning, you had to watch Shelvin for a moment to notice that something wasn't right. As he aged, his shaken brain didn't grow, and his head began to be too small.

I was so sad for Shelvin and for his birth family, including the mother who began shaking him, apparently from the time he was just weeks old. Sometimes, though, my sadness would turn to anger when I saw the constant effort and 24-hour a day care it took to try and keep him comfortable.

Like Jacob, Shelvin was in the middle of everything. He was held, kissed and talked to. He was bathed, massaged and loved. But this boy could only receive.

Shelvin's brain and nervous system were shattered. For months we prayed and watched his face expectantly. Did he hear? Did his beautiful eyes follow motion? Did he respond to us, or was everything involuntary?

As the years went by, we still hoped for healing. His picture was on our fridge, and though he was far away geographically, we loved him and prayed for healing.

God said, "No." Shelvin was never to be healed in this life. His entire short trek on this earth he mostly just received. From a distance, this time, we watched as the McFarland's loved, attended, advocated for, and clung to this precious little flickering flame. It seemed that the world was against him. The family who brought him into the world ultimately ended his life. The social system that stepped in to rescue him proved to be fickle.

Angel Shelvin, by Pastor Darryl Carnley

I will admit the first time I met little Shelvin, I was a tad freaked out. Here is this little black baby without any muscle control just hanging out of Dean's arms like a rag doll. When Dean moved, little Shelvin's head looked like a bobblehead. I loved how Dean acted as if Shelvin was this whole, healthy little guy. Interestingly enough, with Shelvin's physical issues, he ended up being one of the most whole complete human beings I ever met. Shelvin's tragedy that had been afflicted on him by human beings had left his body without use but hadn't changed or altered his God-given essence of setting you at ease and complete peace. Tube-fed and without control over the normal functions of most of his little body, when you walked into his presence, it's as if angels were around him. As I heard of what had been done to him by his parents, my heart hurt, and anger was released into wanting revenge for the stupidity of the depravity of mankind when not guided by the love of God. Shelvin's condition was the product of fallen man but his attitude and the atmosphere he created was that of God's kingdom. When you looked into his eyes, you were soon to see that this life on earth is merely a vapor. You could see destiny in his eyes of another world that holds no grip on the his current situation. When you held him, it was like holding a baby lamb, maybe like the one that was carried back by Jesus from the 99. When Shelvin finally passed away, and I was the honored pastor to officiate his homecoming. The service was the most special service I've ever attended with many people like me who stood and spoke of how this little child affected their life in the most special of ways. Their words were all simplistic in the sense of how being in the presence of Shelvin, there was total peace. You knew you were in the multitude of angels. Just like his funeral service, there was a sense that Heaven's hosts were there in mighty form. As if there was an anticipation of his homecoming and their excitement of playing ball with him or just listening to him speak for the first time. The ultimate God holds all the rights to your spirit and soul. One day when we are over on the eternal shores of Heaven, I'm looking forward to feeling a tap on my shoulder and there stands Shelvin looking at me with those amazing deep dark eyes, and he says, "Waz up?" LOL, I'm sure he will have shorts and flip-flops on, just like Dean, the best dad he ever had. And want to play some kind of boring board game like Kelly, the amazing mom who loved without wanting anything in return. Heaven will be complete!

Footnotes

ADD – Attention Deficit Disorder – Four main qualities are selective attention, distractibility, impulsivity and, in some children, hyperactivity.

AFO – Ankle Foot Orthoses are custom made supports for the lower leg and foot. Used for keeping the foot in alignment.

Alobar Holoprosencephaly – a brain abnormality in which the brain does not divide into the normal two hemispheres. This results in massive brain damage and major system malfunctions. Everything along the midline of the face is affected.

Amniotic banding – a congenital disorder caused by the entrapment of fetal parts, usually a limb or digits, in fibrous amniotic bands while in utero.

Anencephaly – A severe congenital condition in which a large part of the skull is absent along with the cerebral hemispheres of the brain.

Arthrogryposis – A condition involving multiple joint contractures.

Aspiration – A condition in which food, liquids, saliva or vomit is breathed into the airways.

Cerebral Palsy – A congenital disorder of movement, muscle tone or posture.

CINA – Child in Need of Assistance, requires the court's intervention due to neglect, abuse, or a developmental disability/mental disorder, and the parents/guardians/custodian are unable or unwilling to provide proper care.

Cleft palate – Opening or splits in the roof of the mouth and lip.

Clinical depression – a constant sense of hopelessness and despair.

Clubfoot - a term used to describe a range of unusual positions of the foot at birth. The heel is usually smaller than normal and the foot is generally twisted inward and downward.

Cortical blindness – total or partial loss of vision caused by damage to the brain's occipital cortex

Coloboma – A condition where part of the eye tissue is missing.

CPS – Child Protective Services

DFYS – Division of Family and Youth Services

DMHDD – Department of Mental Health and Developmental Disabilities

DNR – A medical order indicating a person should not receive CPR if the heart stops beating. Do Not Resuscitate

FAS/FAE – (Fetal alcohol syndrome, Fetal alcohol effect) A condition in a child that results from alcohol exposure during pregnancy and can include; low body weight, poor coordination, hyperactive behavior, difficulty with attention, poor memory, difficulty in school, learning disabilities, and speech and language delays.

Fixed shunt – Valve that allows CSF (Cerebral Spinal Fluid) to drain when the pressure exceeds a fixed threshold.

G-Tube – Gastrostomy tube – A tube inserted directly through the abdomen that delivers nutrition directly to the stomach.

GAL – Guardian Ad Litem, a person appointed by the court to advocate and represent the best interests of a child in a CPS proceeding.

Hydrocephalus – An abnormal buildup of cerebrospinal fluid in the ventricles of the brain. The fluid is often under increased pressure and can compress and damage the brain.

Hyperacousis – characterized by an increased sensitivity to certain frequency and volume ranges of sound (a collapsed tolerance to usual environmental sound).

Hypervigilance – an enhanced state of sensory sensitivity accompanied by an exaggerated intensity of behaviors whose purpose is to detect threats. It is also accompanied by a state of increased anxiety which can cause exhaustion.

Hypothermia – When the body's temperature falls below 95 degrees F

Interstate Compact – Oregon legislation that mandates that placement must be monitored by ICPC (Interstate Compact on the Placement of Children) when a parent is placing a child in a non-relative setting.

J-Tube – Jejunostomy tube – A surgically placed tube put directly into the small intestine. Feedings are done by pump rather than gravity.

Mic-Key – Low profile feeding tube.

Microcephaly – A condition where the baby's head is smaller than expected, often due to abnormal brain development.

Midfacial cleft – the two halves of the skull fail to join during pregnancy, leaving a cleft or dip along the central portion of the face.

ODD – Oppositional Defiant Disorder – a condition in which a child displays an ongoing pattern of an angry or irritable mood, defiant or argumentative behavior and vindictiveness toward people in authority.

Orogastric tube – A plastic feeding tube that is inserted through the mouth, down the esophagus, and into the stomach.

PFD – Permanent Fund Dividend – A dividend paid to Alaskan residents that have lived within the state for a full calendar year. The amount varies from year to year based on the price of crude oil.

RAD – Reactive Attachment Disorder – Caused by a lack of attachment to any specific caregiver at an early age and results in an inability for the child to form normal loving relationships with others.

RSV – A virus that causes infections of the respiratory tract.

Shaken baby syndrome – a serious brain injury resulting from forcefully shaking an infant or toddler. This destroys a child's brain cells and prevents his or her brain from getting enough oxygen which can result in permanent brain damage or death.

Toxemia – A condition in pregnancy characterized by high blood pressure.

Vas Deferens – Sperm duct

White Coat Syndrome – Anxiety that occurs while a patient is being seen at a medical center. Often causing hypertension.

3/18/2000 Anchorage Daily News

The parents of a Fort Richardson infant hospitalized in November in a permanent vegetative state were arrested Friday on assault charges.

Josette R. Stackhouse, 19, and Shelvin J. Stackhouse, 20, were charged with first-degree assault, a felony that carries a maximum penalty of 20 years in prison, according to the criminal complaint filed in Anchorage district Court.

According to the complaint, baby Shelvin Stackhouse, then 3 months old, was admitted to Elmendorf Hospital on the afternoon of Nov. 30 after his mother called 911 and was later transferred to Providence Alaska Medical Center. Doctors found hemorrhages, swelling of the brain and fresh fractures to a bone in the left leg. They also found four fractured ribs in various stages of healing and signs of a healed broken leg, the document said. A brain scan found a skull fracture and no brain activity.

Doctors said the baby's critical head injuries occurred within 24 hours before his hospital admission. Other than an hour spent at a neighbor's home, he was with his parents at that time, the charging document said.

A week after he was admitted, physicians provided a prognosis that Shelvin would remain in a vegetative state for the remainder of his life, court documents said.

Military police called Alaska State Troopers to assist with an investigation.

The investigation led to the neighbor, who said she watched the baby the afternoon of Nov. 29. She told investigators that the baby cried when he was picked up, had a dazed appearance and slept fitfully, the charging document said.

While at the Stackhouse's' home that evening, she noticed that the baby had raspy breathing and that his eyes rolled back into his head and his legs extended in a rigid manner. She said he needed to go to the hospital. At first, the Stackhouse's agreed, then changed their minds, the documents said.

Josette Stackhouse called the next day to say there was no change, and the neighbor advised Stackhouse to call the emergency room. Stackhouse phoned her two hours later and said she had called a nurse, who told her to place the baby in a warm mist in the shower, the court paper said. Minutes later, Stackhouse phoned again to say she had called 911.

Investigators interviewed a triage nurse at Alaska Native Medical Center who said she received a call on Nov. 30 from Josette Stackhouse. Based on a description of symptoms and after listening to the baby's breathing on the phone, she advised that he be placed in a warm mist for 20 minutes. When Josette Stackhouse called again with more information and said the baby was limp on the couch, the nurse told her to call 911.

On Dec. 8, an officer from Fort Wainwright who was in Anchorage on another child abuse case spoke to Shelvin Stackhouse in the pediatric intensive care uni9t. According to the complaint, he told Sgt. Sean Adkins that the baby had been hospitalized because his wife had dropped him, then shaken him to try to get a response.

The Stackhouse's told investigators they did not know how the baby had been hurt or who hurt him, the criminal complaint said.

The couple was jailed Friday, each in lieu of $100,000.00 cash bail. They were scheduled to be arraigned today.

6/9/2000 Anchorage Daily News

A teenager charged with beating her infant son into a vegetative state walked away from a halfway house last Friday and remains at large.

Josette Stackhouse, 19, took off while emptying the garbage, one of her chores at the Cordova Center, said Cathy Okeson, regional director for Cornell Companies, which owns the center.

Stackhouse was not pursued. People who run away while at the three community rehabilitation centers operated by Cornell are not chased, Okeson said. The centers are not secured facilities, and the staff is not armed.

Stackhouse is not considered dangerous, said officials involved in the case. A warrant was issued Monday for her arrest. Okeson said she is still trying to discover if something specific prompted the flight.

Stackhouse and her husband, Shelvin Stackhouse, 21, were indicted in April on a total of 14 counts of assault. They are accused of breaking their baby's legs, ribs, and arm during a series of assaults and fracturing his skull in November, the day before the injuries came to the attention of authorities. The child, who was three months old when taken to the emergency room at Elmendorf Hospital, had no brain activity.

District Attorney Susan Parkes said the child, whose name is Shelvin Stackhouse, is still alive.

Both Stackhouse's were originally held in lieu of $100,000.00 bail and a court-approved third-party custodian – someone willing to keep within sight or sound of them 24 hours a day. In the Anchorage courts, a third-party custodian is required in nearly all bail situations. However, at hearings after their arrests, judges allowed them to move into separate halfway houses and reduced their bail to zero.

Bail is meant to ensure that defendants show up for court appointments. If they don't, the person who posted the bail, usually a friend or relative, loses it.

Third-party custodians are meant to monitor defendants' behavior while out on bail and to turn them in if they don't follow the rules. It is often easier for a jailed defendant to come up with bail than to find someone willing and acceptable to take on the responsibilities of a third-party custodian.

The combination of the two restrictions is considered an effective hold on many defendants, who might otherwise have to sit in jail for as much as a year while waiting to go to trial.

Halfway houses are meant to be places for sentenced criminals who are nearing the end of a long prison term and need to prepare for their return to the community or who are serving a relatively short sentence, such as those convicted of drunken driving.

However, over the past year, the city's halfway houses have started acting as third-party custodians for pretrial defendants in certain cases, including the Stackhouse's'.

The Department of Corrections proposed using the halfway houses as custodians to help free beds at Cook Inlet Pre-Trial Facility and to keep beds they are paying for at the halfway houses filled, said Superior Court Judge Elaine Andrews. "It's a very welcome option" that "provided more protection to the community than a no institutional third party," Andrews said.

Staff at halfway houses report misbehavior, give random drug and alcohol tests and are awake at night, she said.

Bail is not always zeroed out when a halfway house becomes the custodian, and it's not clear why that was done in the Stackhouse case. Josette Stackhouse's attorney couldn't be reached Thursday. Shelvin Stackhouse's attorney, Sidney Billingslea, said no one objected to dropping her client's bail if he went to a halfway house. However, he was never transferred and remains at Cook Inlet jail, she said.

6/15/2000 Anchorage Daily News

Josette Stackhouse back in jail.

A woman accused of beating her infant son has been returned to jail 12 days after she walked away from a halfway house. A man recognized Josette Stackhouse, 19, walking on Taku Drive on Tuesday evening and called the police, Anchorage police said. Officers arrested Stackhouse walking down Chena Avenue. She was taken to Sixth Avenue Correctional Center and held on $100,000.00

bail. Stackhouse had been staying at the Cordova Center halfway house, which acted as a third-party custodian, as she awaited trial on charges stemming from a November assault that left her then 3-month-old son in a vegetative state. Because she had not been convicted, she cannot be charged with escape, Assistant District Attorney Mary Anne Henry said. Stackhouse's husband, Shelvin Stackhouse, also has been charged in the case.

11/22/2000 Anchorage Daily News

Man enters plea in baby's beating.

A man accused of beating his 3-month-old son into a vegetative state in November 1999 pleaded no contest Tuesday to endangering the welfare of a child. Shelvin Stackhouse, 21, was indicted in April on seven counts of assault along with his wife, Josette Stackhouse. They were accused of breaking the legs, ribs and arms of their baby, also named Shelvin Stackhouse, during a series of assaults and fracturing his skull. Assistant District Attorney Mary Anne Henry told Judge Larry Card on Tuesday that Shelvin Stackhouse accepted a plea agreement that included his testimony at Josette Stackhouse's trial, set for February. The charge of first-degree child endangerment is a felony that carries a maximum sentence of five years and a fine of up to $150,000.00, Card said. The charge included leaving the baby with another person "knowing that the person has previously physically mistreated or had sexual contact with any child and the other person causes physical injury or engages in sexual contact with the child," according to Alaska statutes. He is scheduled to be sentenced in March.

1/8/2002 Anchorage Daily News

A young mother convicted of severely injuring her infant son was sentenced Monday to seven years in prison.

Josette Stackhouse, 21, pleaded no contest to two assault charges in Anchorage Superior Court. Judge Larry Card suspended another five years and ordered her to serve ten years on probation.

Stackhouse denies she did anything to hurt her son, Shelvin, said defense attorney Robert Herz.

Shelvin wasn't yet three months old when he was taken to Elmendorf hospital with severe injuries in November 1999. Prosecutors said the baby was hurt in a series of assaults. Doctors found swelling of the brain, a fresh fracture to his left leg, fractured ribs in various stages of healing and a healed broken leg, according to a criminal complaint. A brain scan found a skull fracture and no brain activity.

Stackhouse and the baby's father, Shelvin J. Stackhouse, 22, were indicted in April 2000 on multiple assault charges related to the injuries. Shelvin Stackhouse pleaded no contest in November 2000 to endangering the welfare of a child in an agreement that included his testimony at his wife's trial. He was a soldier stationed at Fort Richardson when his son was hurt.

Josette Stackhouse's trial was set for this week. She decided to accept a plea offer from the state rather than risk a longer sentence, Herz said. She pleaded Monday to one count of first-degree assault and one count of second-degree assault after giving up hope of regaining custody of her son, her attorney said. She could get out in 2004 with good behavior, he said.

After her arrest in March 2000, Stackhouse walked away from a halfway house, where Herz said other residents were tormenting her. She was caught after 12 days.

The injured child lives with a medical foster family in Fairbanks. The state Division of Family and Youth Services is seeking to permanently sever both parents' rights to him, Hertz said

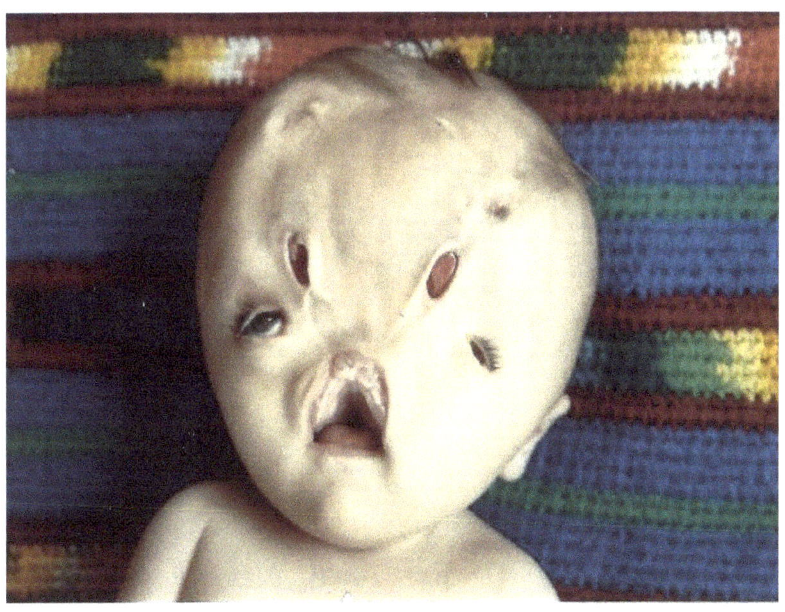

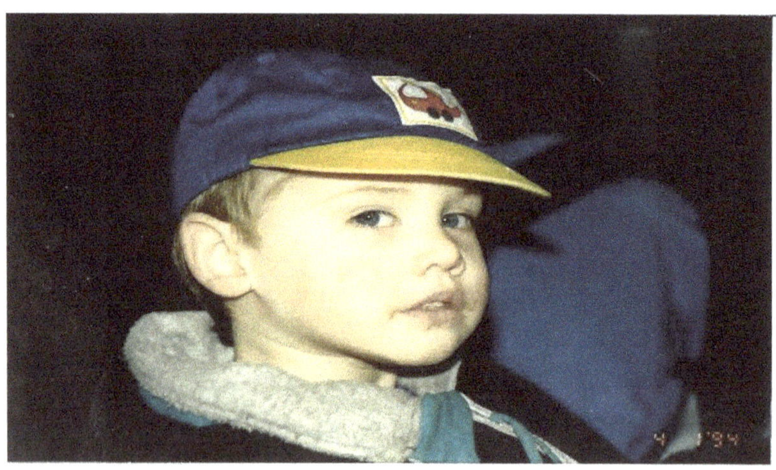

Michelle, Jacob and Keagan

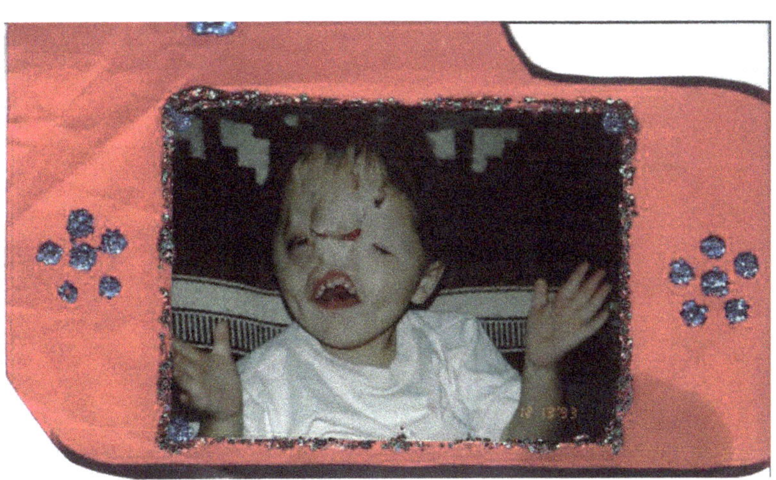

Jacob before and after surgery

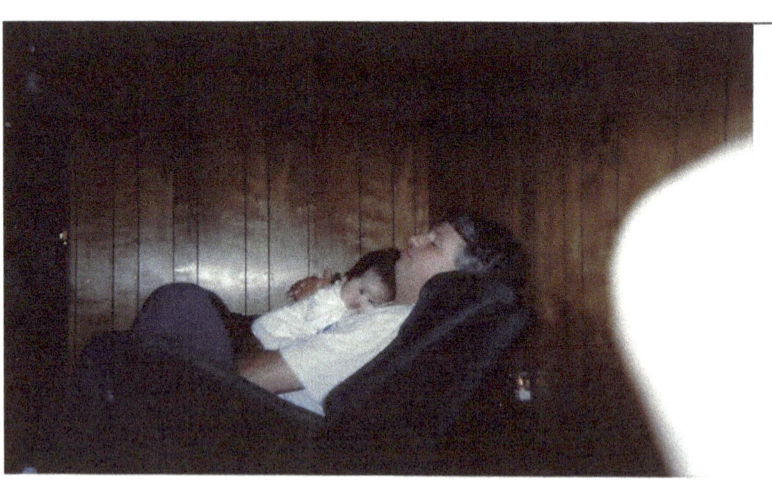

Jenny with Kelly and Dean

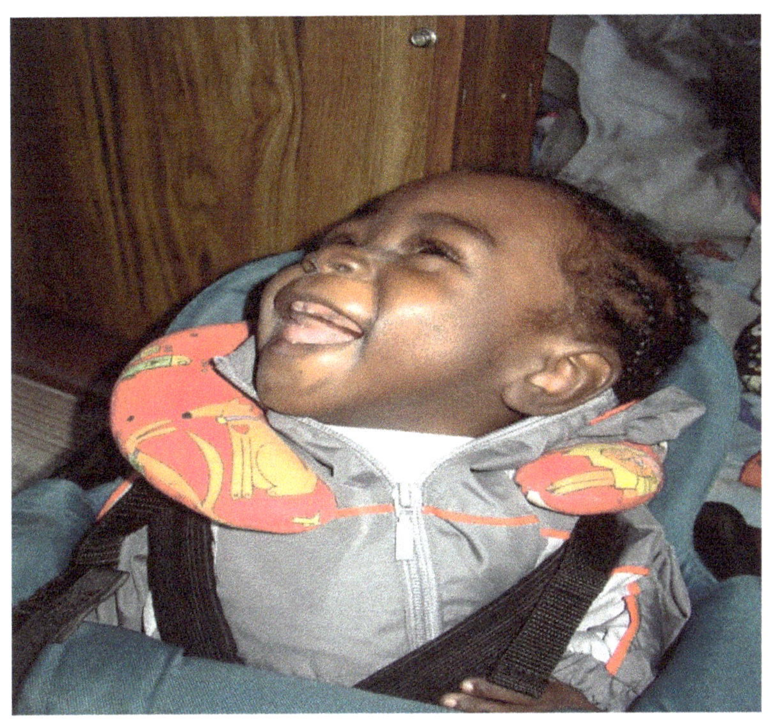

Tony and Keagan

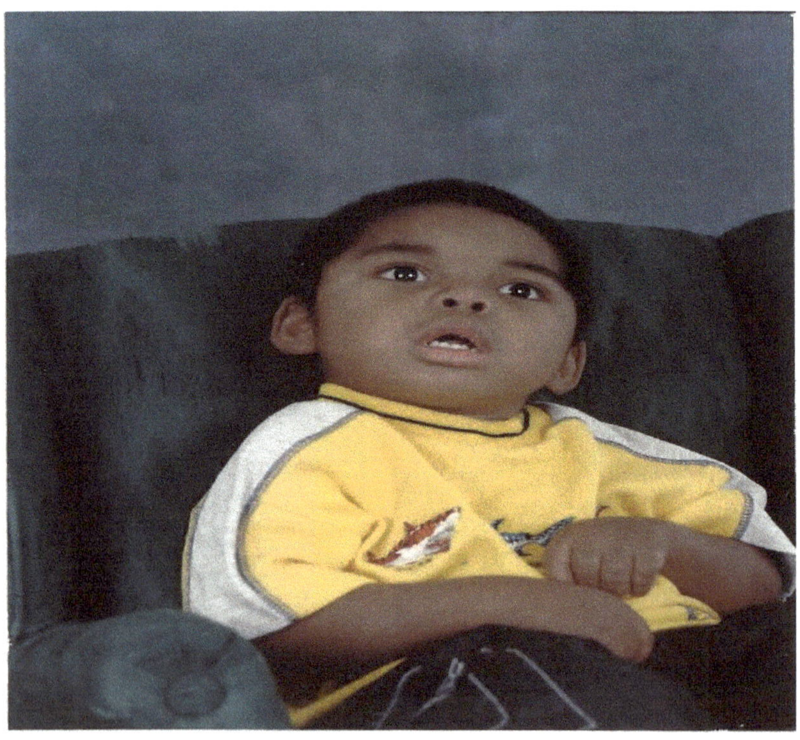

Dean, Michelle and Shelvin

Timeline

80 Married - September

81

82 Michelle –Nov

83

84 Lacy – July

85 Moved to Ketchikan – June

86

87

88 Jacob – Nov

89 Jacob with us – March

Jacob move to WA - Nov

Jacob to Ashley House

90 Keagan – Nov

91

92 Jake returned - June

93

94

95 GAL petition

Jake move to WA – Oct

96 Jenny - Aug

97 Moved to North Pole - June

Jacob died – July

98 Dr. Matt – July

99 Attachment Center – Aug

Shelvin – September

Michelle to Japan – Dec

00 Shelvin with us – Jan

Lacy to us - June

01 Michelle to Africa

02 Lacy to TX - June

03 Africa - April

Lacy pregnant

Keagan & friend burglary

Lacy married - Nov

05 Papa died – Jan

Shelvin died – Mar

Tony

06 Michelle married – Apr

07 #1 grandson – May

08

09 #1 granddaughter – June

10 Mom died – Aug

#2 granddaughter – Dec

11 Keagan to OR

12 Tony died

Moved to Oregon - Sept

13 #3 granddaughter – September

14

15 House fire – Apr

Grandma Margie died – Sept

16 New house – June

18 Michelle moved to TX - Dec

19 Keagan married - Dec

20 Moved to TX

9 798869 116161